Haunted Memories

Healing the Pain of Childhood Abuse

Perry L. Draper

Fleming H. Revell
A Division of Baker Book House Co
Grand Rapids, Michigan 49516

© 1996 by Anita Draper

Published by Fleming H. Revell
a division of Baker Book House Company
P.O. Box 6287, Grand Rapids, MI 49516-6287

Printed in the United States of America

Library of Congress Cataloging-in-Publication Data

Draper, Perry L., 1930–1994
    Haunted memories : healing the pain of childhood abuse / Perry L. Draper.
    p. cm.
    Includes bibliographical references (p.).
    ISBN 0-8007-5573-1 (pbk.)
    1. Adult child sexual abuse victims—Psychology. 2. Adult child sexual abuse victims—Counseling of. 3. Adult child sexual abuse victims—Religious life. 4. Child sexual abuse. 5. Pastoral psychology. I. Title
HV6570.D7   1995
362.7'64—dc20   95-44367

Dedicated to my faithful wife, Anita, my five children, and my seven grandchildren . . . last count.

Contents

Acknowledgments

A special word of thanks to my wife, Anita, whose encouragement through the years has made the completion of this manuscript possible. Thanks also for her inspiration and personal sacrifice through the countless hours of writing—hours that could have been spent in more personally rewarding pursuits.

I wish to publicly thank each of those who assisted in shaping these ideas into a more readable form. Among them are: Barbara Hanrahan, a book reviewer for the Evangelical Church Library Association, for her encouragement and helpful suggestions from the perspective of the general reader; Dr. Scott Schafer, a longtime friend and colleague who added further polish; Randy Petersen, a freelance writer and editor who offered very valuable suggestions for making the manuscript more readable and interesting; Barbara Crouthamel and Ruth Wagner, for help in proofreading, a thankless task that requires attention to detail that I do not possess.

My utmost appreciation and respect goes to those whose case studies are presented here. Each has experienced a great deal of pain and struggle, but all have indicated a desire for others to know their story, to hear their plea. They do not look for sympathy, they just want your understanding, acceptance, and caring even when they don't feel worthy of it. They have been willing to risk sharing their story

with you, coming from the past when no one dared speak
of these things.

Perry L. Draper, D.Min.

As Perry was near the completion of this book, he frequently said, "I am never going to finish this book." The
day he ran off the last chapter on our laser printer, I unexpectedly had to rush him to the hospital. In a couple of
hours the Lord took him home. Though he died of something like a stroke, he had always had low blood pressure.
So it took us by surprise.

His book has a different approach to abuse, and he had
such a burden to get this message out to the people. Therefore, a group of us banded together to follow through and get
it published. I am so appreciative to this group: my children,
my pastor (Rev. Joel MacDonald), and Randy Petersen.

In addition to those already mentioned as having helped
to make this book possible, there were two who helped me
to be more objective in going over the galleys. They are Barbara Hanrahan and Carol Lang, a New Jersey licensed marriage and family therapist.

Anita Draper

Introduction

Although a seasoned counselor for more than two decades, I was not prepared for the flood of adults in the past five years seeking help with horrendous memories of childhood sexual abuse. I was directly confronted with a massive problem in our society that heretofore only occasionally touched my awareness. Although most of my clients are from a Christian orientation, a rapidly increasing number of these same people were reporting severe traumas from their early years that still held a vise grip on their minds, emotions, and relationships. They painfully recounted unspeakable incidents of sexual molestation, abuse, and incest.

Somewhat naively, I did not expect to find this problem in the Christian community. I was wrong. I could understand such a problem in families sadly lacking in moral teaching and understanding, but not among the supposedly faithful who knew and believed differently. What was going on?

Nor were my clients talking about some isolated event in their lives, to be discussed briefly and left behind in distant memory. For most, there were *repeated* atrocities in their young and tender years, not from strangers, but from people they loved and respected within the extended family, or someone well known to them. Their experience was far more than an unfortunate event in their lives. They endured devastation of such tremendous proportions that it had deadened their inner spirit beyond that of any other life experience I had ever heard or witnessed. Their hearts were broken and bleeding. Their trauma had isolated them from the mainstream of society. They had no one to whom they could turn.

The purpose of this book is to share their stories with you, the Christian reader, that you might understand them, their plight, their need for a helping hand. Their names and some case material have been changed to protect the identity of the individuals. They want you to hear their message. They will spare you the worst of the details but they want you to understand, not only for them, but for children present and future who could be protected from this terrible plague among us that has been rampant and unchecked for so long.

As I sought to help clients deal with the effects of childhood sexual abuse, I was forced to review the events of my own life. Although I had not thought much about it or defined it in quite the same way, I too had experienced sexual abuse as an early adolescent. Although I had worked through a lot of the deep feelings that had invaded my own life, I had never adequately connected them with their origins in my own abuse experience. Rather, I had looked at the whole thing as a dark chapter of my life to be acknowledged and then moved on. Certainly that long ago, *nobody* ever talked about such things. A taboo subject, to be sure. I had no idea there were so many others fighting the same battle. I will share some of my own experience and pain, to help personalize the message of this book, for I too have lived most of what is here and have found the way of healing and deliverance available to others as well.

Whether you are a pastor, counselor, Christian worker, or someone interested who wants to be helpful, this book will assist you in grasping the seriousness of the struggle of survivors of sexual abuse. Friends and family may also find some help in understanding someone they care about. Therapists will find the book useful to share with their clients. I am sure that survivors of abuse will find the material of very real value as well.

This kind of recovery issue is not popular, but it must be faced. Its victims cannot be abandoned. They need you to hear and understand. Nor can any of us afford to put our heads into the sand and ignore those among us who so struggle. The problem is not the individual survivor's alone. The problem is ours together, for it impacts each one of us.

Part 1
The Hidden Problem

1

The Secret

All my longings lie open before you, O Lord;
  my sighing is not hidden from you.
My heart pounds, my strength fails me;
  even the light has gone from my eyes.
My friends and companions avoid me because of my wounds;
  my neighbors stay far away.

Those who repay my good with evil
  slander me when I pursue what is good.
O LORD, do not forsake me;
  be not far from me, O my God.
Come quickly to help me,
  O Lord my Savior.

Psalm 38:9–11, 20–22

Janice was greatly distressed. Her words came only with great difficulty between sobs. Haltingly she began to pour out the story of her favorite uncle. They had done many fun things together when she was young. Janice had always looked forward to visiting with him. However, one day things began to change. Her uncle introduced other "play" that disturbed her greatly. Clutching more tissues, she struggled on.

"He began to touch me in private places," Janice stammered. "I was confused. I didn't know what was going on. It didn't seem right, but he said this was something that good friends do if they love each other. I was too young to know what it meant."

After a long pause, Janice took a deep breath and went on. "He did more," she sobbed. "Each time I was there, he went a little further. Each time he told me it was our special thing, and that no one else should know about it, because they could not share the same love we have for each other. I was in need of hugs as a child, but not all this. Still he was the adult; I was the child. I didn't know what was going on."

Janice reached for more tissues as she prepared to go on. She squirmed in her chair. She cringed as she told me how he aggressively seduced her into overt sexual acts, not once, but again and again.

"I was so scared. I just wanted to die! All I wanted was love, someone to care, and he turned it into something awful. What happened to the fun times? Where did it all go wrong?" A flood of tears followed.

"When it was all over, he gave me the line again about our special love, and left me alone in my grief and pain. How could he do this to an innocent child?" she cried. Janice dried her tears.

"And that is where I have been ever since, alone in my grief and pain. I have never shared this with anyone before," she blurted. "Can you help me? I am so confused. I feel terrible."

Janice was in a great dilemma. Although her home background did not provide the kind of loving atmosphere she needed, her favorite uncle seemed to be genuine in his caring. He filled some emotional empty spots, but his initial sexual advances left her confused, unsure what to do. She sensed this was not quite right but was powerless to resist him. He was so big, and she was so small. When she did try to complain about what was happening, he reminded her of all the things he had done for her, and that she was very dear to him. This was their "special secret." Assuming that adults must know better than she, the twisted relationship continued. Over time the uncle became bolder and more aggressive, carefully drawing her into further exploitation. Janice had attempted to tell her mother what was happening but was not believed. Instead, the mother chided her for saying such things about the uncle who was well respected by the family. He couldn't possibly do anything like that! She must be imagining things!

Now an adult, Janice anguished over the memories and a multitude of emotions that went with it. She tried hard to forget the whole thing, to put it behind her forever, to get on with her life. The harder she tried to forget, the more it welled up from within.

Slowly depression and anxiety began to creep into Janice's life. She felt down and discouraged. Sometimes she found herself crying for no apparent reason. Day-to-day problems seemed to loom larger than ever. The future seemed too dark to even think about. Feelings of fear, shame, worthlessness, anger, hurt, and confusion grew. The daily struggle of life became more difficult. Worry and anxiety were gaining the upper hand. Her problems seemed to be getting worse with time.

Janice desperately needed a friend. She had a burning desire to share her experience with someone, but who? As a child her efforts to tell someone were misunderstood and had left her feeling isolated from others. She was hesitant to trust again. Not even her friends were aware of what lurked in her background, only that she was a bit shy and quiet. Her secret remained tightly locked within, and her difficulty relating to others became more acute. Janice suffered alone.

A Real Problem

Janice's story is no isolated incident. Others just like her have come to my office as they have to other therapists across the country. It has been my privilege to help those who have come to me with their struggle. Little by little the feelings came out, memories returned. I agonized, wept, and grieved with each one. Their anguish was real! This was not some figment of their imagination or something they dreamed up just to get sympathy. Their battles were deep and genuine, coming from the inner core of their souls. They courageously struggled through feelings of self-hatred and blame, cried in their confusion and betrayal, and agonized in their deep pain. I felt for them as they desperately reached out for someone to genuinely care, someone just to accept them as they were, without condition. They seemed to have no one who understood the depth of their pain, no one who cared enough to hear them out, to believe their message, to accept them, to love them as they were. I could not ignore their suffering. I could not turn them away. Janice and a host of others like her are hoping that you will not turn away either.

The Silent Cry

The problem of childhood sexual abuse is far worse and more widespread than most of us would imagine. And there are reasons why. Incest and sexual abuse are not popular subjects. Most people do not want to talk about them. In fact for years, even centuries, the problem of abuse has been kept hidden, only an occasional incident ever making it into the open. It was a taboo subject. Only in the last few years have public figures spoken out about the problem, disclosing only bits of their own abuse. Others are following suit, and the world is now beginning to hear of what has been going on right under our noses for so long.

Why haven't victims talked about their abuse in the past? Why have they kept silent? Certainly they have suffered enough. Why have they been afraid to speak? Why have they kept it such a tightly guarded secret? All those I have spoken to felt very trapped by fear, stuck in a no-win situation in which it was far better to suffer silently than to suffer the consequences of revealing the truth. Consequences for revealing the truth? Definitely.

Unbelief

One important reason for silence has been unbelief on the part of significant adults. Many victims have tried to tell a parent or an important caretaker, only to be rebuffed. Instead of understanding, help, and protection, the victim has heard such reponses as:

"You're imagining things. How could you possibly think something that terrible could be done by such a caring and respected person? Forget it, you're just making that up."

"You bad girl, you must be doing something to make this happen. Shame on you."

"Nobody will ever want you now. You've been ruined for life."

"Oh, forget about it; it's not that important."

"Well, if it happens again, tell me about it." (And nothing is ever done about the problem even though it happens again and again.)

The child's sense of betrayal by his or her own caretaker becomes yet one more victimization that springs the trap shut. Can you picture a young child being blamed for seducing an adult? What young child wants to try again with those kinds of responses? The abuser is believed; the child is not.

Fear of Reprisal

A second reason for silence lies in the fear of reprisal, that the victim will be hurt, beaten, or even killed if he or she tells anyone. Many young victims fear for their lives if they do say anything. The abuser is too big and frightening for a young child to put up much resistance. The adult is just too powerful.

The abuser may also threaten the victim's family. He or she may tell the child that parents or other loved ones will be harmed or even die if the child tells.

Power Games

In cases where there are no physical threats, there are other power games designed so that the victim loses every time. The abuser may use such phrases as:

"This is our special secret together. We don't want anyone else to share this, do we?"

"We have a special kind of love that we don't want anyone else to know about."

"See, you liked it. You're just like me. You're bad."

"After all the things I've done for you, you wouldn't want me to look bad or get in trouble, now would you?"

The child has few options in an adult world. The more compliant the child, the easier it is for an abuser to control the situation, maintaining the secrecy of the guilty abuser at the expense of an innocent child.

Family Consequences

Another reason for secrecy is that of family consequences. The child's security is wrapped up in the home, and the parents who act as caretakers. No child is ready or able to face the outside world alone. If he or she fears that the home will break up, someone will go to jail, or the family would be thrown into too much turmoil, the child may choose to suffer the abuse and thus keep some semblance of togetherness. Such messages as this are common:

"If you tell about what we are doing, I could be sent to jail. You don't want to make that happen, now do you? How would the family make it financially? You wouldn't be able to stay in this house any longer. Do you want to be responsible for breaking up our home and family?"

> "If the authorities ever find out, they will put you in a fos-
> ter home away from your family. You don't want that
> to happen, do you?"
> "Your mother doesn't want me in bed with her, and that
> leaves me very frustrated and discouraged, like I don't
> even want to be here. But you make me very happy
> with our special relationship. I don't know what I
> would do without you."

These statements may sound bizarre, but they are said.
Some children will actually sacrifice themselves to keep the
family together. A young child would rather be beaten or
sexually abused than in some way contribute to his or her
home splitting up and the family's security being shattered.

Shame and Embarrassment

Some victims don't talk because of their own deep sense
of shame and embarrassment. They think thoughts like
these:

> "How could I have let this awful experience happen to
> me? Why didn't I put an end to it sooner? There must
> be something wrong with me. I must be really stupid."
> "I must be an evil person for this to happen. What did I
> do wrong? Certainly no one could love me if they ever
> found out."
> "I feel like such an awful person. I'm not worthy of other
> people's time and attention. I'm better off alone where
> I feel safe from hurt and rejection from others."

Scorn of Peers

Some victims, particularly boys, are afraid of being
laughed at by their peers or being considered wimps for letting such a thing happen to them. They are confused as to
whether they were molested or this was simply a sexual experience common to most boys. They have fear and confu-

sion as to whether this now means that they are homosexual (if the abuser was a male).

Bill kept a tightly guarded secret. As a young boy he was not readily chosen to be on the teams at recess. He did not feel fully accepted by his peers. However, a friend of the family took an interest in him by spending time to help upgrade Bill's skills in sports so that he could be more accepted. Bill loved the attention and was indeed improving his skills.

At the same time, however, his new friend and helper began to teach a few other skills that weren't part of the bargain. He began to show Bill soft-core pornography. At first, there was something strangely exciting about this new activity. Later the man began to play with Bill's genitals, praising him for what a fine boy he was. Bill was confused, not knowing how to respond to this man who had been a very helpful friend.

The man skillfully led Bill on to other sexual experiences. Bill did not know how to stop all this. He felt powerless and very ashamed. Now he not only was afraid to talk about what was happening for fear he might be blamed for starting it, but he was also afraid he would be a homosexual for life. A frightening thought! The secret remained carefully tucked away. Bill struggled to fit in with others but found it very difficult.

Marjorie was a very attractive, intelligent, and talented young lady. As she struggled to tell of her stepfather's repeated abuse from age five on through her teen years, she related how he repeatedly threatened to kill her with his chain saw if she did not give in to him. She was afraid, for she took his threats seriously.

When Marjorie tried to tell her mother what was happening, her mother turned on her, accused her of being a whore, and refused to help. It was all Marjorie's fault as far as the mother was concerned. The mother had little to do with her daughter from that time on. She severely restricted Marjorie's activities, not even allowing her to take part in programs for honors she had earned. The mother blamed Marjorie for everything and basically treated her like dirt. The mother's allegiance was clearly to the stepfather in spite of his longtime abuse of her own daughter.

Only when as a late teenager Marjorie saw her stepfather begin the same kind of reprehensible behavior toward her younger sister did her fear turn to rage. Marjorie then garnered the necessary strength to report the abuse to a teacher at school. The stepfather went to jail, and the mother became even more infuriated with Marjorie, making her life miserable.

Indeed the obstacles are many. Without an encouraging and accepting environment, the truth will never be known. Victims are extremely cautious to whom they reveal their deep inner struggle, no matter how desperate they are. They search for someone who will

listen
understand
accept them without judgment
keep their confidences very private
walk with them through their pain
share their heavy load
encourage them when they get discouraged
help them know what *normal* is
be their loyal friend

Summary

Some who are reading these words have never before given serious thought to the problem of childhood sexual abuse. Although you hear about it in the media, you are not personally aware of people with that kind of trauma in their lives. Therefore, the problem seems distant, remote, and irrelevant, and not something you need to be concerned about. Their pain does not touch you directly.

Others may choose to ignore the problem because it is too unpleasant. "I don't even want to think of those terrible things," some say. "I don't want the awful pictures of their trauma in my mind. Don't tell me about it."

I would challenge you as a reader to be willing to learn, to set aside your past opinions, and to look hard at a great host of suffering people around you who need your encouragement. I would invite you to read on and hear their messages. They will spare you the worst of the details.

If you, the reader, have been molested in your past, I would encourage you to take heart. Health and happiness are within reach. Just as a host of other victims are finding help and healing, you can as well. I would encourage you to read on, to understand the extent of the far-reaching damage that has been inflicted on so many areas of your life, and to find the path of healing.

2

The Problem

Keep on loving each other as brothers [sisters]. . . . Remember . . . those who are mistreated as if you yourselves were suffering.

Hebrews 13:1, 3

During my twenty-five-year ministry in Christian counseling, I have always worked with victims of childhood sexual abuse. Their number was not large, but they were very needy. In the past few years, however, the number of victims has greatly increased. Suddenly my work drastically shifted from family counseling to counseling survivors. This did not necessarily mean there was a dramatic increase in the number of people being abused, but rather a large number were now coming forward with trauma from their past that they had never dared to share with anyone. Their ages at the time they entered my door ranged from late teens to fifties, but most have been between thirty and forty. They have told me of sexual abuse situations of all kinds—some mild, some very prolonged and severe. For some it started at unbelievably early ages and continued for a long time. For others the problem came later, after puberty. It seemed like a stampede of very troubled people that was not about to diminish.

Definitions

What is sexual abuse? Dr. C. Everett Koop has given a very clear definition:

Child sexual abuse occurs in a child—any person under the age of 18—who is made to engage in, or to help someone else engage in, any sexually explicit conduct, such as intercourse, sodomy, the fondling of genitals, and oral copulation.

It also occurs if the child is molested, raped, is involved in incest, or is sexually exploited, as in child prostitution or pornography.

A child is abused if he or she is enticed, bribed, threatened, or coerced in some way, particularly by force, to engage in any of these acts, or if the child is developmentally not old enough or mature enough to understand the consequences or implications of these acts.[1]

Mic Hunter, author of *Abused Boys, the Neglected Victims of Sexual Abuse,* states that violence or threats may or may not be overt components of the abuse. In other words, the sexual contact is still abusive even if the adult behaves in a gentle manner. Adults only infrequently need to resort to actual physical violence to be sexual with children. More often, enticement, rewards, misuse of authority, or misrepresentation of what is taking place is used instead.[2]

When the victimized person is a child, often the term *child molestation* is used. When the child is molested by a relative, it is called *incest. Sexual abuse,* the more general term, is in fact a sexual act that cannot be ignored. In most cases, it is not the touch itself but the meaning behind the touch that is harmful. Sexual abuse can be an expression of power, compulsiveness, a desire for control, or an act of vengeance, which often comes masked as an act of love.[3]

As Jill recalled painful memories of incest by her father, she could picture the look on his face. Instead of the love she longed for, she saw anger, arrogance, and the aura of power—he knew he had her under his control. Any attempt to resist was met with increased power on his part. His strength was too much for her small size. He seemed to take great pleasure in her helplessness and his ability to overpower her.

She could respond only with hurt and a deep well of pain. How could a father who claimed to love her take such great pleasure in hurting his daughter in this way? He had to have power over her before he could be satisfied.

Misunderstandings and Myths

Why isn't more being done about this problem? Why have we let such abuse go on unchecked for so many years? Why have so many victims found no protection from the predators of society? Why have we done so little?

Part of the difficulty lies in a vast amount of misunderstanding and myth about sexual abuse. Perhaps because no one really wants to think about the subject of sexual abuse, and most of us would like to make it disappear altogether, it has been easy to accept popular myths without question. Mic Hunter points out some general misconceptions we need to consider:

MYTH: Children are most likely to be sexually assaulted by a stranger.
FACT: 75–95% of offenders are known by and may be related to the child.

MYTH: Children lie or fantasize about sexual activities with adults.
FACT: In developmental terms, young children cannot make up explicit sexual information—they must be exposed to it; they speak from their own experiences. Sometimes a parent will try to get a child to report sexual abuse falsely. Primary indicators of such a report are the child's inability to describe explicitly or illustrate the act, or a grossly inconsistent account.

MYTH: The sexual abuse of a child is an isolated, one-time incident.
FACT: Child sexual abuse is usually a situation that develops gradually over a period of time, and occurs repeatedly.

MYTH: Nonviolent sexual behavior between a child and adult is not emotionally damaging to the child.
FACT: Although child sexual abuse may involve subtle persuasion rather than extreme force, nearly all victims will experience confusion, shame, guilt, anger and lowered sense of self-esteem, though they may reveal no obvious outward signs.

MYTH: Child molesters are all "dirty old men."
FACT: In a recent study of convicted child molesters, 80% were found to have committed their first offense before age thirty.

MYTH: Children provoke sexual abuse by their seductive behavior.
FACT: Seductive behavior may be the result, but is never the cause of sexual abuse. The responsibility is with the adult offender.

MYTH: If children did not want it, they could say "stop."
FACT: Children generally do not question the behavior of adults. They are often coerced by bribes, threats, and the use of authority.[4]

MYTH: When a boy is sexually abused, the act is perpetrated by male homosexuals.
FACT: Most child sexual abuse is perpetrated by men who are heterosexual and do not find sex with other men at all attractive. Many child molesters abuse both boys and girls.

MYTH: When a boy and a woman have sex, it is the boy's idea, and he is not being abused.
FACT: Child abuse is an act of power by which an adult uses a child. Abuse is abuse; a woman abusing a male child is still a child abuser.

MYTH: Males who are sexually abused as boys all grow up to abuse children sexually.
FACT: Only a portion of abused boys go on to abuse children.[5]

As Christians, we must ask ourselves: Why do we avoid the subject? What are some of our own myths and misunderstandings?

One of our myths could be *denial*, "It doesn't happen here. I don't know a single person in my church who has been through anything like that." Don't be so sure. The fact is that most victims of abuse are not likely to tell you about it, but that certainly doesn't mean the problem is not there. Don't kid yourself. I would guarantee there are several victims of abuse in your church, but they haven't revealed it to you. Nor are they likely to let you know until they see a genuine interest on your part.

Another reason Christians might be blocking the problem is because so many are *uneasy discussing sexual issues*. We think it is not a "spiritual" topic. A careful study of Scripture will reveal otherwise, as sex and sexual desire were created by God to be channeled in wholesome ways. Only the perversion of sex is evil. The perversion does not come from the victim but from the abuser. Try to see how the innocence of childhood has been twisted and perverted by another and be willing to look at the long-lasting effects on the child victim. Accept the victim as God would accept him or her, not as someone with a contagious disease that needs to be avoided, but as a wounded child who needs our compassion and love.

Perhaps another reason Christians are uneasy with the subject of sexual abuse is because we are *uncomfortable with anyone in deep pain*. It disturbs our comfort level. We need to have life in neat and easy categories that we can handle. When we meet someone who does not fit into our preconceived ideas, who does not seem to respond to the usual reassurances, we tend to move on to someone else. We may assume the victim does not have enough faith to appropriate the promises of God, or that the victim is not a true believer after all. We may be quick to judge, too quick to turn away and assume the victim only wants to dwell on the past. We thus ignore him or her and leave the victim in his or her suffering. "After all," we muse, "if the victim would just turn his or her life completely over to God, this problem would pass." If we only knew how much the victim wants to do just that and get past this horrible nightmare. If we only knew how many have cried out to God for deliverance from their suffering, to be released from their burden and to be helped to move on. If we really knew, I don't believe we would hold on to our simplistic views for very long.

Misunderstandings abound, but a problem that affects all of us just does not disappear.

Statistics

Just how widespread is this abuse problem? Are there many more than we might normally realize? The statistics are *frightening!* One of the most meticulous studies on the frequency of childhood sexual abuse was conducted by A. B. Russell and C. Mohr-Trainor[6] in the San Francisco area indicating that 38 percent of the 933 women in a random sample had been sexually abused before the age of eighteen, and 16 percent had been abused by a family member.[7] One national study conducted with two thousand adults by the *Los Angeles Times* uncovered sexual abuse among 27 percent of the women and 16 percent of the men.[8] A study by the Canadian government and by the Canadian Gallup Polls interviewed two thousand people of various ages and found that one-third of the males had experienced some type of sexual abuse as a child.[9]

Statistics show that abuse by fathers and stepfathers actually constitute no more than 7–8 percent of all abuse cases, even though it dominates reports from the child welfare system. Abuse by other family members (most frequently uncles and older brothers) constitutes an additional 16–42 percent. Other nonrelatives known to the child (including neighbors, family friends, child care workers, and other authorities) make up 32–60 percent of offenders. Strangers (the traditional stereotype of child molester), who make up the remainder, are in almost all studies substantially less common than either family members or persons known to the child.[10] Of these, only 2 percent of the cases occurring within the family and only 6 percent of the cases outside the family were ever reported to the police.[11]

Because of the fact that many do not report what has happened, or may define it quite differently, there may well be multitudes more. We just don't know at this point. Often males have more difficulty identifying themselves as abuse victims when the offending person is a woman, because society traditionally sees the male as the one responsible in such cases.[12] Often adult male abuse of boys is lumped in the realm of homosexuality or is considered to be "experimentation" and not correctly defined as abuse, and therefore it is not reported. None of these assumptions are correct.

According to Dr. Grant L. Martin, misconceptions are also present within the church community. The evidence suggests the incidence of sexual abuse is every bit as high in Christian homes. Admittedly, the data is limited, but the informal evidence of the extent of abuse within the church is very convincing. Though it is difficult to measure someone's level of Christianity, many counselors, therapists, and researchers do report that among churchgoers the adult male offenders tend to be very devout, moralistic, and conservative in their religious beliefs. In Dr. Martin's talks with college counselors, therapists, researchers, and personnel at sexual assault centers throughout the West Coast and Midwest, the conclusions are unanimous. The rate of sexual abuse is *no less* in religious or Christian homes than in secular homes. One counselor from a Christian university told me a major portion of his caseload of students was for problems related to sexual abuse.[13]

A study completed at Fuller Graduate School of Psychology surveyed nine hundred Christian counselors and pastors on the subject of family sexual abuse. The majority of those who responded to the questionnaire felt that incest occurred as often in Christian as in non-Christian homes.[14]

Dr. Martin also quotes significant people in the field. He reports that Dr. Henry Giaretto, founder of Parents United, the nation's largest treatment center for incest victims and their families, while acknowledging the lack of hard data, affirmed that the most serious cases in his program have come from the highly dogmatic, religious family. Dr. Bob Rencken, director of the Family Development Center in Tucson, Arizona, also verified the overrepresentation of rigidly religious fathers involved in incest. His experience, based on a large multidisciplinary treatment program, is that a typical offender is likely to have a rigid, highly structured, religious style. Often the offender is extremely regular in church attendance, but with no sense of community or participation in the fellowship of the church. Other data suggests that there is a tendency for offenders to be strongly opinionated, with an outspoken view of right and wrong, regardless of behavior in private. Richard Bitumen, professor at Whitney College, describes incestuous fathers as coming from all areas of society.[15]

Now that a more receptive social climate prevails, and survivors of childhood sexual abuse feel more able to speak, they are showing up in great numbers in therapists' offices and hospitals all over the country. The data suggests that severe childhood abuse may play an underestimated role in the development of many serious psychopathologies heretofore given other diagnoses or causes. Numerous well-documented studies done since 1987 indicate that 50–60 percent of psychiatric inpatients report childhood physical or sexual abuse, or both.[16]

So what does all this mean to you and me? Simply this: *For every one hundred people in your community, church, or organization, you can expect to find more than thirty women and about fifteen men who were molested before the age of eighteen.* Now that is frightening! If sexual abuse were a biological disease, it would be declared a major epidemic of catastrophic proportions. The whole country would be mobilized toward treatment and prevention of any further outbreak.

A problem of this size demands that you and I face it squarely. As unpleasant as the problem may be, none of us can afford to put our head in the sand and hope it will go away. It just won't disappear. Each of us must face the problem in whatever way it might affect us. First we must understand it, and then we must try to do whatever we can to stop it and to help its victims. That is the challenge I put to you.

Summary

If you are not ready to hear the story of victims of sexual abuse, or you lack intestinal fortitude, you won't know who the victims are, you won't understand their problem, nor will you be in a position to be of help. You will be unable to do anything to stop this awful plague on our society until you first understand what it really is. If the statistics mean anything at all, you already know several survivors, possibly someone near you right now. They are in all walks of life, and their number is large. The problem is not going to go away without your help and mine.

Part 2
Extensive Damage to the Person

3

Interruption of Normal Growth and Development in Early Childhood

My heart is in anguish within me;
    the terrors of death assail me.
Fear and trembling have beset me;
    horror has overwhelmed me.
I said, "Oh, that I had the wings of a dove!
    I would fly away and be at rest—
I would flee far away
    and stay in the desert;
I would hurry to my place of shelter
    far from the tempest and storm."
                            Psalm 55:4–8

Childhood sexual abuse is a crime against innocent victims who do nothing to cause it. Further, the extensive and long-lasting effects of that crime produce years of suffering that few understand. From the very first trauma of sexual abuse in a child's life, a chain of destructive events begins to take shape that interrupts normal growth and development. Twisted ways of thinking and feeling are introduced that will affect the child for many years to come. In order to make sense of the vast amount of inner turmoil, the victim needs to understand the process of change in thinking, believing, and feeling that results from severe trauma. A major interruption in the child's development takes place, producing lasting effects for years to come.

Childhood Developmental Needs

Vital to understanding the effects of sexual abuse on a child is the fact that normal growth and developmental milestones are short-circuited. The sense of being loved and protected, so basic to normal development, has been interrupted and twisted by the perverse behavior of an important adult in the child's life. As a result, the child grows up severely stunted in emotional and spiritual development.

Every child goes through a whole series of developmental learning tasks as a natural part of growing up. In the physical realm, such basic skills as the ability to sit up, to feed oneself, to crawl, then to walk become the focus of the first year or so. Then follows increasing speech ability and toilet training. Learning appropriate behavior begins as the young child learns the meaning of the word *no*. The child learns to put words together and develops communication skills.

Socialization with peers begins when the child first learns that there is benefit in sharing his or her toys. The young child learns that the world does not revolve around him or her. The arrival of a new sibling brings the message home quickly, not to mention the fact that important adults no longer dash to and fro attending to his or her every need. The child begins to learn that there are many people in his or her world who have expectations and demands, and not all of these are consistent or clear; some are quite confusing, and some can be rather intimidating and threatening. The child expects his or her parents to provide protection from the danger of known and unknown evils.

Emotional needs are likewise present throughout the developmental stages. In infancy a child can express anger, pain, hurt, fear, insecurity, and self-centered demands communicated mostly through crying. This seems perfectly acceptable to the child. Amazingly, a little wailing generally makes the significant adults snap to attention, and the parents become motivated to respond. Positive parental response to the young infant builds trust, security, and a sense of being loved and cared for. As the child grows, the same emotional needs for love, encouragement, affirmation, protection, and the sense of being important to someone remain vital to a normal, healthy emotional life. Having those needs met may become somewhat more complicated, as infantile demands are no longer acceptable.

Spiritual values are added as time goes on. The child learns that the world is bigger than himself or herself, that there is someone greater than his parents. Out there is a Creator who has made the world of trees, flowers, rivers, lakes, oceans, the animals, the sky, sun, moon, stars, and days that follow one another without fail. The child learns that we are not alone, and that each of us answers to a power greater than ourselves.

The child grows in his or her understanding of values that are vital to life—not just a sense of what is right and wrong, but what is good, what is bad, what is better, and what is worse. The child absorbs what is really important in life, the main goals to be sought after. All these are learned first from the parents, who become the most important influence, but later from the extended family, then from peers, other authorities, and the media.

Any major interruption of the various developmental milestones brings unhappy or even disastrous results. Sexual abuse is a devastating interruption to development. The damage done to a child who has been sexually molested will have far-reaching effects for years to come. Generally speaking, the younger the child at the onset, the duration and frequency of the abuse, the amount of force used, the closeness of the abuser relationally, the number of abusers involved, and the response of significant others, all add to the long-range damage to the child. This chapter gives but a glimpse of the early effects on the abused child.

Confusion

Consider the child, in most cases around seven to nine years of age, who normally looks to his or her parents for security, love, emotional support, protection, and caring, but at the same time is being exploited sexually by a parent. All normal physical and emotional boundaries have been broken. What do we have now? *Confusion*. The child cannot explain what is happening, much less why.

Children at this young age are not normally sexual in their thinking or actions. Therefore, a young child who has been molested for the first time is quite innocent of what is going on, has certainly not invited it, and has no previous information to know how to understand or evaluate what is happening. Add to this the fact that most young children trust their parents implicitly and thus do not believe parents are wrong. So if the abuser is a parent, the child will believe that it must be his or her own fault. But what did he or she do to cause this? The child doesn't know.

The child is very confused by the fact that the person the child loved, trusted, and depended on has betrayed the child and treated him or her with callous disregard. Similar confusion and sense of betrayal come if a family member whom the child had trusted was unwilling or unable to protect or believe the child.[1] The child will not understand what is really happening, only that something about this whole experience is not right, and shouldn't happen. But the child won't know what to do about it. Threats of harm for divulging the secret or negative consequences to the family only serve to heighten the confusion. Being beaten into submission or brainwashed by the older and more powerful adult makes it all worse. How can this be love?

Add to this the child's natural, self-centered perspective. The child needs to explain his or her world in terms of "what *I* did wrong." "After all," the child reasons, "this shouldn't be happening in the first place, and so it must be my fault. But I don't know how to fix the problem."

Next add a new and insidious thought pattern that begins to take shape. The child now learns that love from a parent, relative, or family friend involves some sort of sexual activity. Love and exploitation become welded together. As abuse continues, the child unconsciously accepts that all relationships are meant to be this way. Any loving relationship from this time forward will include the concept of exploitation, being used by another for his or her personal gratification. Little else can be expected in life.

Normal emotional growth is now short-circuited. Trust is shattered; love is twisted; safety is gone. The child is emotionally stuck and unable to grow in any normal fashion. The confusion remains for years to come.

Jennifer came from a troubled home. As she grew up, she tried hard to be the person her parents expected. Although she was not aware of her earlier years as she began therapy, little by little her memories revealed a mother who was very emotionally abusive. Not only was there no positive emotional support, Jennifer received severe criticism and punishment for every little thing. Nothing she did was ever right. Jennifer felt extremely inadequate throughout her growing-up years. Jennifer's father was a distant, passive man, who was hardly involved in the family at all. He paid little attention to what was going on.

Jennifer's uncovering of more memories brought out the painful fact that her brother had repeatedly forced her into sexual intercourse. To make matters worse, he repeatedly invited his friends to join in the "fun." Any resistance on her part was soon forcibly overcome. They laughed at her pain and agony and made fun of her weakness. It was horrible.

As Jennifer approached her teen years, she sought refuge outside the home, turning to her church for solace. Since she was such a needy kid, the pastor began to take a special interest in her. Jennifer welcomed his attention as an answer to her prayers. Soon, however, the pastor showed too much interest in her and was beginning to make sexual advances to her. What a bitter disappointment!

Being a bit older and a little wiser, Jennifer was able to get out of that situation before it went very far. She felt betrayed and very much alone. One single message bored its way into her innermost being: "No men can be trusted." That was the clear message of her life's experience up to that point. No wonder trust became a major issue in her healing process! The normal ability to trust in relationships had been severely shattered and would affect every relationship of her life from there on.

Because the child views the surrounding world as being the same as the world within the immediate family and its close circle of friends and relatives, the child will assume that everyone else in the world is the same. "If this one person I really trusted betrayed me and no one else supports me in my grief," the child reasons, "then there must not be anyone whom I can trust."

Vulnerability

Not all children are *forced* into sexual abuse. Many children are of a very compliant nature. They have a strong need to please others, especially adults. They may already be emotionally hungry because of parental deficiencies. Being the compliant, obedient kids that they are, they may be neglected simply because they don't complain. They try hard to make everything go smoothly, hoping that in turn they will be accepted and loved. The opposite tends to happen. Because compliant children don't complain or make much noise, others tend to forget that they are around, assuming they are getting along just fine. Indeed, they may well be very needy emotionally, much more so than the strong-willed child who is always making a fuss.

The quiet but emotionally needy child, then, becomes an easy prey for the chronic abuser. Because the quiet child will try hard to please the adult, an abuser can readily entice the child by meeting some important emotional need the child exhibits. Once the abuser has won the child's trust and confidence, he or she may then move slowly into the realm of suggestive pictures, pornographic material, touching of private areas, and eventually into complete sex acts. The abuser is careful at the same time to continue giving positive emotional strokes to the child. What a deadly combination!

The child's need for love and attention and the child's sincerity and need to please have all been seriously warped and compromised by the abuser. The child is stuck again. Many years will come and go before all this will get sorted out.

Sam was neglected at home. His father was never available for him during his growing-up years. The father's mental illness kept him from normalcy, sometimes able to work, sometimes glued to the couch, doing absolutely nothing to help out at home or to support the family. When Sam needed his father's attention or wanted to show him something that he had created, the father just couldn't pull himself together to look. Sam would try very hard to design and build things that would make his father proud, but the father never showed any interest. Sam's efforts were to no avail.

Sam's mother had risen from a difficult background also, and she found little time for her children. She was an intense person, rarely relaxed, was given to a temper, and deeply resented the father's immobility. The combination of these two factors gave Sam little emotional support at home. The family grew, but none of the siblings developed closeness with each other either. One sister was helpful at times, but she had her own life to lead and her own problems to deal with.

To make matters worse, Sam did not fit in well with his peers. He was quiet, timid, emotionally needy, never knowing how to connect with others socially. He was often picked on, was made the subject of jokes by others, and was generally misunderstood.

In early adolescence, Sam was befriended by one other boy about his age. Eventually his new friend introduced him to an older boy he already knew, and the three went off to isolated places to seek new adventures. Things began to happen that Sam was not prepared for. His new friend and the older boy began to do sex acts together. Sam did not enter in at first, but he soon saw that he was being ignored and ridiculed for not becoming a part of their "fun." Because of his own deep need to be accepted and to be important to somebody, Sam soon got involved. Some of it was new and exciting, some of it was downright disgusting, but he did have some feeling of importance at last.

Although Sam never felt right about the whole thing, the sense of belonging was too hard to pass up. He was too emotionally needy to refuse. It was all too easy to get more and more involved until the passions consumed his life. It was the pits, but now it was too hard to quit. Only as time went on and Sam got sufficiently angry and disgusted with himself and his friends did he finally crank up the courage to get away from them and look for something more constructive to do with his life.

Low Self-Esteem

Everyone who has survived the ravages of sexual abuse struggles with low self-esteem. The sense of being *soiled and spoiled* comes through clearly.[2] Victimized children all seem to have a deep loathing of themselves. They believe they are ugly, stupid, hateful, disgusting, worthless, and will never amount to anything. They have come to despise their bodies, and believe that everyone else is just as repulsed by them as they are by themselves. They believe they must indeed be evil persons to have done all the things they have. They cannot accept themselves in any way, and all the convincing of others to the contrary is totally in vain. They do not believe others could ever accept them, for they cannot accept themselves.

A good, healthy view of oneself as a person is vital to normal life, affecting every area of our personal happiness. Sexual abuse undermines the victims' self-confidence and short-circuits their emotional growth. Stuck again.

Marjorie recoiled and withdrew as I tried to convince her she was a bright, attractive teenager with many talents—all of which was true. The very thought of any positive characteristics was totally foreign to her, and she did not trust or believe what she was hearing. She rejected any belief that she could ever be a whole person and find fulfillment in life as others do. She sincerely believed she was ruined for life, and that there was no prospect of ever reaching any worthwhile goals. The fact that she was at the top of her class and had won several honors made no real impact on her.

Being rather artistic, Marjorie occasionally brought drawings she had made to her therapy sessions. One of the early ones was that of a young child, obviously very sad, lonely, unhappy, and admittedly unattractive. She vigorously denied the drawing was of herself. As her therapy progressed, as she worked through the traumas of her own experience, and as she began to find the real person underneath the ruins and rubble of her life experiences, the drawings began to change. The child became older, still somewhat tentative and lacking confidence, but nevertheless greatly improved.

Near the end of her therapy Marjorie again brought a drawing, this time of a beautiful young lady with flowing hair, full of poise and confidence, stunningly attractive. Again she denied that she had drawn herself, but she admitted her views of herself had changed. Marjorie now had a bright future; she had important goals for a useful life that would make anyone proud. She had even tried some dating, gone to a few parties, found herself well accepted, and enjoyed the occasions. She had turned an important corner.

Joe had a low opinion of himself for years. Because relationships were distant, cold, and empty in his own family background, he never felt loved. Although he had friends in the community, both peers and adults, and was well accepted by them, the same empty feeling gnawed away inside.

Joe found a job with a man in the community who was developing his property and needed a young person to help him out part-time. This new endeavor went well for a while until the man started introducing Joe to sexual things, a bit at a time. Each experience was new, exciting, and very fascinating, although Joe never felt quite right about it. The personal attention filled Joe's emotional hunger, and there was always a little more to keep his interest.

Joe liked to please people and found it hard to refuse an adult, but as the exploitation continued from bad to worse, he had increasing internal conflicts about this relationship. He knew it was wrong and went against everything he knew about right and wrong. Only after a lot of agony and increasing degradation was he able to finally put a stop to the abuse. However, the inner feelings about himself gnawed away for many years to come.

Although the resulting confusion of this unhappy relationship interfered with his concentration in junior high school, Joe had a desire to better himself through a college education. As the strength of his determination gathered, Joe took the challenge of getting good grades in high school so that college could become a reality, and he graduated near the top of his class. Learning new things became a lifelong quest. College followed, then seminary, Christian ministry, and other adventures, but the low self-esteem continued to gnaw away inside.

Only after he had completed his third graduate degree did it finally dawn on Joe that perhaps, just maybe, he did indeed have some kernel of intelligence after all. What a revelation! An important milestone had been reached in accepting something positive about himself.

Socialization

Fitting in socially becomes a major hurdle for those suffering from sexual abuse. They feel different from others and sincerely believe no one could possibly understand them and their struggle. Deeply rooted in their social difficulties are their feelings about themselves and their low self-esteem. Because of deeply implanted views about self, victims of abuse will literally withdraw from most social contacts, prefering isolation because it is more comfortable. They do not want the focus of attention on themselves and will hang on the outer edges of the group, hoping they won't be noticed.

For adolescents, the prospect of gym class, and having to take open showers where they can be seen by peers, is terrifying. They are very self-conscious about their bodies. They expect total rejection or ridicule. They feel very inferior in every way and just want to hide. Some would rather fail gym than subject themselves to such torture.

Unfortunately, because they withdraw and keep as low a profile as possible, their fears become self-fulfilling prophecy. Quiet kids are not that well understood. Some peers will recognize that a quiet, private kid just wants to be left alone and will accommodate by ignoring him or her. Others take the quietness and withdrawal as being stuck up, conceited, and superior. Consequently, what follows is not understanding at all but hostility. The victim of sexual abuse then becomes the victim of taunts, jeers, name-calling, false rumors, and exclusion by peers. The child feels more a victim than ever. What few friends he or she may find are usually at the bottom of the heap, fellow underdogs, and subject to similar treatment.

Without realizing what he or she is doing, the victim of abuse unconsciously contributes to more abuse and further victimization. Because of being a loner, seeming different and weak, and acting like an outcast, others read this as if there were a sign on his or her back that says, "Kick me, for I am worthy of your abuse, and that is my lot in life." Thus the cycle of abuse in one form or another is reinforced again and again. The victim of abuse continues to take what is dished out, feeling helpless to fight back. The problem goes on and on.

Whatever sense of loneliness he or she felt before is now further exaggerated. Abuse by someone the child has learned to love is one thing, for that creates a tremendous sense of rejection and loneliness in itself. But a whole life of personal loneliness seems to lie ahead with no real hope for change. Many throw themselves into their schoolwork, music, arts, activities, or anything to keep themselves busy and ignore the gnawing emptiness deep inside. Again, the child is stuck.

> Sam was a very quiet boy. Hardly anyone got to know him, and few got many words out of him. He always hung back, staying on the outer edges of any group. He never volunteered to do anything, thinking that he could never be as good or do as well as someone else. He kept hoping he would never be put on the spot. He hated to participate in class, since he was very afraid of giving a wrong answer and being laughed at by his peers. Because he was so quiet, he was often overlooked by peers and adults.
>
> Some of the more aggressive boys picked on Sam and gave him a rough time. Sometimes they pushed him around; sometimes they punched him; other times they called him names. He felt terrible, but it was easier to withdraw than to stand against the onslaught. No one understood Sam's pain, and the fear of exposure made it too dangerous to be himself. So he suffered alone, for that was safer.

Only years later did Sam understand that life did not have to be this way. He learned that his own poor self-image kept him trapped in an unnecessary prison, that his assumptions that others could not accept him were false, and that he could attain a fulfilling life after all.

4

Early Childhood Effects

Pain and Anguish

The cords of death entangled me;
the torrents of destruction overwhelmed me.
The cords of the grave coiled around me;
the snares of death confronted me.
In my distress I called to the LORD;
I cried to my God for help.
From his temple he heard my voice;
my cry came before him, into his ears.

He reached down from on high and took hold of me;
he drew me out of the deep waters.
He rescued me from my powerful enemy,
from my foes, who were too strong for me.
They confronted me in the day of my disaster,
but the LORD *was my support.*
He brought me into a spacious place;
he rescued me because he delighted in me.
Psalm 18:4–6, 16–19

We have looked at several of the early effects of childhood sexual abuse on the young child, but there are more that go even deeper that we should understand. In this chapter we will discuss the anger, guilt, shame, confusing sexual arousal, and deep inner pain that can damage the child's very soul.

Anger

Everyone I have ever known who has been subjected to child abuse suffers from a deep well of anger that has no legitimate outlet for expression. There is so much to be angry about: for being betrayed, used, and deprived of one's childhood. The anger is readily joined with fear: fear of further retribution if the child resists, or fear that his or her anger will get out of control as that of the abuser. "If I get angry, I will get hurt." The more emotionally impoverished the child, the more there is to lose by a display of anger.[1] The anger has nowhere to go.

As the anger burns, it may just smolder within. As the incidents of abuse are repeated again and again, the trapped anger builds in pressure and intensity. Occasionally there are angry outbursts that seem out of character for this quiet, gentle child. People are momentarily shocked, but the one with the deep well of anger becomes more fearful. Because the child is already emotionally impoverished, he or she is afraid of losing what little love might be available and, therefore, forces himself or herself to repress the inner anger. Furthermore, the child is afraid the anger will get out of control, that it will pour out like a raging torrent and hurt someone. The victim clamps the lid down tighter to ward off the new danger. The inner pressure builds even higher.

Because of the strong tendency to blame self for everything that happened before and now, the child victim of abuse is unable to explain where all this anger is coming from. "Now I am really sure there is something seriously wrong with me," the victim will think. "No good Christian is supposed to be this angry." Therefore the child buries the anger within. He or she is now angry at himself or herself for having all this anger. The repressed anger may now turn into depression, and depression digs its own self-defeating hole. An endless cycle takes over, plunging the child deeper into despair and a hopeless sense of powerlessness. The lack of positive information to help offset all this negativity only serves to make the problem worse.

For some victims the anger could have become an ally, but they don't know that. Many child abusers back off when they see anger displayed, and they become afraid to further pursue their evil plans. Indeed, a number of potential victims have warded off attempts by would-be abusers simply by displaying anger and feistiness. Other victims are not so fortunate, however, either because they are too young to know what is going on or are physically forced or beaten into submission by someone much larger and stronger than themselves.

As Jill worked back through fragments of her memories, feelings of anger began to surface. Angry feelings surprised and scared her. They were unfamiliar, as she had kept most of her anger carefully suppressed out of fear. She had seen her father beat her brothers with that terrible belt, and she wanted to avoid the same kind of treatment at all costs.

Although her earlier memories told her that she loved her father a great deal and related to him far more than to her mother, feelings of intense anger and hatred were now making themselves known. She struggled with an intense sense of betrayal, that a father would treat his loving daughter as a piece of dirt, a body to satisfy his lust. How could it be? All she wanted were hugs and assurance that she was special to him in a wholesome way. Instead, he had taken away the innocence of her childhood and ruined her future.

Jill distinctly remembered how her father would use his belt to beat her into submission if she resisted. Next he would tie her hands to the headboard of the bed to render her helpless. He then started his ugly ritual of sexual exploitation. She vividly pictured his face with eyes leering at her. She felt enraged; she hated him. She wanted to kick him in the face. But the fear was too great, and she was too small. She could not risk it. The anger remained buried deep within.

Guilt

All survivors feel loads of guilt. Most adults will have difficulty understanding why an innocent young child who was clearly manipulated or forced into abuse will feel such vast amounts of guilt for something the child did not cause. The roots of the problem remain in the child's view of what happened. Children look up to parents and older adults, even older kids, and therefore do not question the motives and actions of their elders. Children believe that if something is really wrong in the relationship, it must be their fault. Young children are not yet developmentally able to sort out what is right and wrong about sexual acts. They only know that somehow they were involved in it, it wasn't right, they didn't stop it, and so they must be to blame.

The child has never really put together the fact that he or she did not cause this, even when beaten into submission. "I must have done something to deserve the beating," the child reasons. Even when the truth is explained, the child still cannot accept his or her own innocence and is quick to support the adult abuser's actions. "I must have done something wrong," the child affirms. The heavy weight of guilt does not readily change but remains stuck for years to come.

One thing that does seem to modify the child's viewpoint is if the child sees the abuser try the same abuse on a younger sibling. At that point, the older child can see the picture more clearly and may well act to protect the other sibling by coming forward with the truth. The child is now able to reason more clearly and seems to say, "It may be okay to abuse me, but you have no right to abuse anyone else."

Although Marjorie could not figure out what she was doing wrong for her stepfather to repeatedly force her into sexual relations over many years, she was thoroughly convinced that she was completely to blame. No arguments on my part seemed to make a dent in that wrong belief.

However, when Marjorie had reached her late teens, the stepfather's attentions began to turn to a younger sister. Once Marjorie saw what was coming next, she went straight to a teacher with the truth. The authorities took over from there, and the stepfather ended up in jail.

As I reviewed Marjorie's actions with her, and her intervention on behalf of her sister, I was able to help her see the truth. Marjorie recoiled at the idea that her sister could have acted in any way to seduce the stepfather. Never! Her sister was not like that. He was! When I then asked her how she could blame herself, as she was in the very same situation at an even earlier age, the light began to dawn and the wall of guilt and self-blame began to crumble. Marjorie could now see the point. She was no more responsible for her stepfather's actions than her sister was. The light of truth began to pierce the blackness.

Shame

Beyond the guilt goes an even deeper feeling: shame. Sexual abuse is always a very degrading experience. In its worst form, forced incest at an early age is totally devastating! Every victim I have known feels tremendous shame, embarrassment, humiliation, and degradation.

Mic Hunter views shame as the most powerful and damaging emotional effect of sexual abuse.[2] Guilt can be handled with difficulty; shame is too overwhelming. Guilt says, "I have done something wrong, a specific, identifiable *act*." Shame says, "I am a *terrible person*. I deserve your rejection because there is nothing good about me. If I had been a good person, none of this would have happened." Shame reaches into every corner of the victim's personality with its message that everything about the child is bad, evil, hateful, and unworthy.

On the surface, low self-esteem and shame may seem to be the same. Indeed, it is a deep sense of shame that drives the low self-esteem. Low self-esteem is the weed that is visible above ground, but shame is the root that keeps the low self-esteem alive and flourishing. The child's acceptance without question that he or she must be an evil person feeds the feelings of incompetence, self-loathing, and withdrawal. Because the child has no one to provide the love, caring, and support so desperately needed to help offset the tremendous damage, the child remains stuck in a deep sense of shame.

As a fellow survivor, I recalled similar feelings about myself in early adolescence. Although most would have seen me as a kind, obedient, and responsible boy, I felt awful about myself. I was very active in my church each week without fail and well thought of by peers and adults, yet I did not feel right inside. I not only felt this continual sense of guilt for having done something wrong, but I also believed I was the worst sinner in the world. I believed that somehow people must know that something about me wasn't right. If I was criticized for doing something wrong—anything at all—I felt tremendous guilt and shame. I was a worthless person. How could anyone love a person as awful as me? How could I accept any kind of caring or love from another? I was too unlovable.

I developed a strong defensive wall to prevent anyone from getting to my inner self, to touch my deep sense of awfulness. I was always on guard, staying cool and aloof so that no one could find this huge sore spot within. I felt very small and insignificant, totally useless, and very vulnerable. Nothing would relieve the awful aching within. Recovery from shame would be too difficult. It would take too long to get back on my feet again.

Arousal

Normally a young child does not experience sexual arousal unless somehow previously exposed to it. The child is basically in a stage of sexual innocence that remains until puberty, at which time sexual urges can become confusing enough. The child is not developmentally ready to handle the powerful force of sexual arousal, does not understand it, has no knowledge of how to control the situation surrounding it, and is generally bewildered by what is happening. Yet because all of us are sexual beings, these urges can be awakened long before their time by a clever abuser who knows just what stimulates those urges and how to bring out that desire.

The child does not know that when he or she is stimulated by another, sexual response is biologically automatic, not something the child caused. The child does not understand his or her own sense of excitement and the strong pull to do more. No matter how much the victim has come to hate the whole experience of abuse with all of its horrors, there lies somewhere within an infectious excitement, which is later recognized as sexual arousal and consequent sensual pleasure. The child again blames self. "How could I ever have felt this excitement or allowed this to happen? I must really be evil." Such arousal brings a tremendous sense of confusion and shame.

Consider the fact that the majority of abused children are first subjected to sexual activity between the ages of six to nine years. Children have very little knowledge of the powerful force of sexuality, its appropriateness, or morality. Little wonder they are confused. Some new force within their own bodies is stirred up and remains in heightened awareness from that time forward. In God's design, sexual expression was intended within the boundaries of marriage, both for procreation and to express the deep love a husband and wife have for each other. Any sexual expression outside of the marital context perverts sex from its original design. The child is caught in conflicting emotions caused by innocence, confusion, guilt, love, hate, embarrassment, and betrayal.

The child is not aware of two major points:

1. Sexual abusers are very powerful people compared to the child. While some use force to coerce the child, the majority entice the child through clever persuasion, playing on the child's innocence, trust, loyalty, and curiosity. The child does not realize he or she is being manipulated and does not see where this will all lead, nor does the child have any real defenses against it.

2. Any human being, child or adult, if subjected to certain physical stimulation, will become aroused. All the abuser has to do is to begin physically stimulating the erogenous zones of the child, and arousal just happens automatically. The child does not have to do anything to respond; it happens naturally. The child knows nothing about how to stop the process; thus the abuser has a tremendous advantage.

The arousal persists throughout childhood and on through adult life. Later, as a teenager or adult the victim may act out the very same experiences of childhood without realizing what he or she is doing, thus bringing greater complications and confusion into his or her life.

Joe did not understand what was happening. This man was his friend, but he was taking Joe down a track he wasn't really comfortable with. First it started with personal questions about Joe's penis. Then it went to pictures of nude women, then pictures of adult sex acts. Next there was touching and physical stimulation in private places. This was all new to Joe. A whole new world was opening that he didn't know existed. Each time he was exposed to this sort of thing, some powerful feelings began to well up inside of him that he couldn't explain.

This new inner force brought an urge for more and more. What was happening? His adult friend led him on in measured steps knowing full well what he was doing. Joe's inner arousal became stronger and stronger with each experience and occupied an increasing place in his mind.

Eventually Joe's friend introduced him to other forms of sex, and exquisite pleasure followed. The whole experience was disgusting but at the same time intriguing. Joe was hooked. He had a tiger by the tail and didn't know how to safely let go. Joe was greatly troubled by his strong urge to go back and allow it to happen again and again. Certainly he had to be causing this in some way, or so he thought. Finally, as his Christian convictions grew stronger, and as he gained more inner strength, Joe was able to gather the courage and put a stop to the whole thing no matter what the man might say or do.

With great relief, Joe thought it was finally over, and he could now move on with his life. But permanent scars from the experience remained. He struggled with the feelings of anger, guilt, and shame, to be sure, but he also began a lifelong struggle with a very high sex drive that cried out for expression every day of his life. What was he to do?

Fortunately Joe's Christian faith and its value system kept him from going too far, but every day was a battle. There were some close calls in dating relationships that could have led to disaster. The guardian angels were busy. Only in marriage to a dedicated Christian wife did Joe find a natural outlet, and even then it took a long time before sexual expression in marriage became an act of true love.

As Jill struggled through memories of her abuse, one overwhelming feeling always came up. It scared her every time. She was deeply embarrassed. Her anxiety level went sky-high. Arousal, that awful arousal. Why was it there? Where was it coming from? She didn't understand. She thought this made her an evil person to have such strong feelings. Jill did not understand that abusers are masters at manipulation and know how to use natural bodily responses to stimulation as a way of drawing the child into totally inappropriate sexual expression.

As more memories of abuse at very early ages came back to her, Jill realized that while she was bound and unable to move, her father would stimulate her to the point of sexual frenzy so that she would beg for relief. He would sexually use her and then would beat her because she "enjoyed" it. The awful arousal had now become stuck within. She hated the feeling but couldn't get free from it.

As a young boy, Rich did not really understand what was going on within him. A girl in her late teens had repeatedly lured him into her secret place. There she skillfully stimulated him, exposing herself to him, eventually drawing him into intercourse with her. Rich did not understand his own sexual responses that seemed way beyond his control. How could he be doing this? But any time he got near her, a strong urge within him took over, and he was drawn to her body and to the sex acts she desired. He found himself looking forward to their meetings, dreaming about them, wanting to meet her again and again. He was hooked. He had lost control, the urges were too strong, and he was so young. She had drawn him into a deep pit of despair by manipulation of natural sexual responses. The excitement of the arousal had become intoxicating—far too much for a young boy to handle.

Inner Pain

Those who have never experienced abuse in earlier years will have difficulty grasping the victims' depth of inner pain. Those who know it firsthand have difficulty describing it. They feel tremendous, excruciating pain deep within their soul. Some have attempted to describe it as similar to having your insides ripped out. Most of the time the pain is kept well hidden and defended behind their personal wall. To let someone near the pain would be very frightening, for this is their most vulnerable spot of all.

People can be cruel. Some have made light of the victims' personal pain; some have not believed the victims; others have laughed in their face or made fun of them. Still others have taken advantage of their vulnerability and driven them deeper into their pain and isolation. Even well-meaning persons may add to the problem by trying to minimize the pain, shifting attention away from it, imposing guilt trips for not having enough faith in God, or blaming the victims for personal sin that must be causing all this suffering.

At the root of the pain is the deep sense of *betrayal.* Finkelhor and Browne present betrayal as one of the four major factors of trauma for victims of childhood sexual abuse—the realization that a parent or trusted person has manipulated them through lies or misrepresentations about moral standards, that someone they loved has treated them with callous disregard. Being disbelieved should the child report the abuse adds further to the sense of betrayal.[3]

Often the very person the child trusted and sought out for reassurance instead exploits the child's weakness for the abuser's own selfish purposes. The abuser does not care if the child is hurt in the process but only thinks of his or her own ego needs for power or gratification. The child feels great pain for being repeatedly exploited by a supposedly loving adult. To make matters worse, the abuser takes great pride and satisfaction in having abused the victim. All this is too much for the child to handle, and the child becomes traumatized.

It is heartrending to hear the cries of the abused or witness their anguish. Guiding victims through the minefield of their inner pain and deep hurt is the most difficult and draining part of helping them to recover—to see it in their eyes and on their face, to feel their overwhelming grief, to hear their unanswerable questions. They cry out to God, "Where were you? Why did you let it happen to me? Why didn't you stop the person? Don't *you* love me either?" Such is their grief. Words will fail at such times. There is no simple way to make it better. Pious platitudes are useless. Only the comfort of a genuinely caring person can be of help.

Oh, yes, I do believe abusive people will receive their just rewards, either in this life or the life to come. Yes, I do believe God was there. He said he would be (see John 16:33). Yes, I believe God helps each of his own to endure and survive. But that doesn't remove the pain; it's still there every day of the person's life. It hurts deeply, and no amount of gentle persuasion will make it go away.

As we listen and try to come to grips with the deep inner pain witnessed in the life of an abuse victim, there is far more than grief and tears. Even though we see an adult person before our eyes, we are actually hearing the wails of an inner child whose heart is breaking. Someone whom the child loved has betrayed a trust and ruined his or her life.

> As I listened to Sally try to express the hurt and pain, she found extreme difficulty in putting it into words. The only thing she could describe was a severe pain in the depths of her chest. It was unbearable. If only she could make it go away. Sometimes she would have impulses to stab a knife into her chest to make the pain die. Her intent was not to kill herself but to make the terrible pain go away. She couldn't stand the horrible pain.
>
> What Sally was trying to describe was nothing other than a broken heart! Many others just like her beg for relief and healing.

Summary

Few understand the tremendous damage of childhood sexual abuse to its young victims. Where there should have been loving support, protection, affirmation, encouragement, and affection, instead the child has received exploitation, manipulation, blame, physical and emotional abuse, twisting of love into sexual perversion, betrayal, and deep inner pain. Instead of developing self-confidence and ability to take on new and emerging tasks of life, the young child remains stuck in the mire of confusion, self-hatred, helplessness, isolation from others, buried anger, tons of guilt, overwhelming shame, perplexing sexual arousal, and the deep inner pain of a broken heart. The child has indeed been traumatized and remains stuck at this point in time in his or her emotional growth.

The challenge each of these victims would put to you is that you take the time to understand their inner confusion and pain or the repetitive cycle of self-hatred fed by the victims' need to explain the tragic events of their lives by blaming themselves. They have been robbed of their childhood and are left with little knowledge of what normalcy is. A part of them has been thrust all too soon into an adult world, and part of them is developmentally stuck as a child in their trauma. Deep feelings of anger and shame, mixed with the confusion of arousal, well up within, long before they understand what these feelings really are. They have come to expect exploitation from others. Demonstrate to them that you are different, that you genuinely care.

The experiences and suffering of each of the persons mentioned here were a journey into hell that few can understand. Many thought they were dying—sometimes physically, sometimes emotionally, sometimes spiritually. Indeed, many felt already dead inside. But the journey is not over. These are only the early effects of the damage. Many long-term effects carry over into adult years. All of this has to be worked through to find the journey back.

5

Later Effects in Adult Life

The Individual

O Lord, do not rebuke me in your anger
or discipline me in your wrath.
Be merciful to me, Lord, for I am faint;
O Lord, heal me, for my bones are in agony.
My soul is in anguish.
How long, O Lord, how long?
Turn, O Lord, and deliver me;
save me because of your unfailing love.
No one remembers you when he is dead.
Who praises you from the grave?
I am worn out from groaning;
all night long I flood my bed with weeping
and drench my couch with tears.
My eyes grow weak with sorrow;
they fail because of all my foes.
Away from me, all you who do evil,
for the Lord has heard my weeping.
The Lord has heard my cry for mercy;
the Lord accepts my prayer.
All my enemies will be ashamed and dismayed;
they will turn back in sudden disgrace.
Psalm 6

Jennifer came to my office after many years in Christian service abroad with her husband and children. Most of her life had gone along reasonably well until recently.

"Why do I feel like this?" she asked. "I have tried very hard to live a life of sincere faith and dedicated service to God. What is happening to me? My whole life is coming apart.

"I feel very down and discouraged—and very confused," she continued. "I have no idea where it is coming from. Can you help me?"

At this point Jennifer was struggling valiantly with a great deal of personal confusion, depression, and anxiety, and she had no clues whatsoever of what was going on. She knew that she must conquer the problem, or she would not be able to return to her God-given ministry of many years. She could no longer cope with the demands of everyday life. She appeared close to a nervous breakdown.

The real causes of the problem were not at first apparent. It was hard to get any kind of handle on the problem. However, as we began to dig below the surface, the problem slowly began to emerge. Bit by bit difficult memories began to surface. Each session was agonizing.

Out of the fog came painful memories of a mother who was emotionally very cruel. Then she remembered an older brother who had many times forced her into an incestuous relationship and had brought his friends in to rape her also. In fact, the whole family was seriously dysfunctional.

Jennifer came to realize that she had come through her early years the best of all her siblings. Her way of dealing with all of those horrible experiences was to block them out of her mind completely, forget them, leave them behind like a bad dream, and press on. The frequent act of shutting out the pain and myriad feelings that went with her abuse was her defense for survival. Repression of her memories had gotten her through those difficult years, but permanent damage had remained. Like a crumbling foundation that would need serious repairs or else the house would come crashing down, the foundations of Jennifer's early years had to be repaired or everything important in her life would fall apart around her.

Repressed Memories

Depending on the extent of abuse in the background, some survivors of childhood sexual abuse will have very clear memories of just what happened to them, and those memories will remain clear throughout their lives. Others will have little recollection of what happened. Generally, the younger the age of the abused, the more extensive the damage, and the closer the relationship of the abuser within the family, the greater the amount of repression of past memories.

I meet an ever-increasing number of survivors who have no conscious memories of their abuse. They come to therapy for other problems. When I ask about memories from their childhood, they either have huge gaps in memory or no memories at all of their childhood. The huge gaps of memory may give important clues that many difficult things happened in their growing-up years that they could not handle, and the mind has blocked the recall to help them survive the terrible experiences. Therefore, survivors can go on for years completely oblivious to the awful past with nothing concrete to connect present difficulties with previous traumatic events.

I often liken the process of repression to what many of us do when unexpected company comes. We quickly scan the house for anything undesirable lying around. We swoop up kids' toys, any orphaned clothes, and miscellaneous junk we can find. We hurriedly stuff them in the closet, close the door, and forget about them. The scene repeats itself again and again. Eventually an insidious problem develops. The next time the closet door opens—you guessed it—many things begin tumbling out. There's no more room there.

So it is with repression. We can only stuff so much into our unconscious mind as the years go by before things start coming out again and demand attention, ready or not. By that time, we not only have a large collection of problems that we have never dealt with, but we have never developed the skills to deal with anything head on. Double trouble.

The task of digging out repressed memories can be a long, arduous task. (See chapter 8, pages 142–44, for a discussion of the whole problem of memory gaps and some of the current debate on that topic.)

Many survivors of sexual abuse have disconnected from the cause and effect of their early experiences of mistreatment. They try to push the past out of their mind—viewing it as a horrible, unhappy experience they want to leave behind—and press on to better things in life. They may not even think much about their past for a number of years. As young adults there are many other things occupying their minds: finding a marriage partner, getting established in a career, starting a family, and working out the many details involved in getting launched in the adult world. Being still young, they have extra energy to help them over the rough spots and keep moving ahead.

A few years down the road, life gets more complicated, and repeating patterns of behavior emerge. The survivor becomes increasingly unhappy and unfulfilled, sensing that something is wrong. Repeated periods of depression appear; anxiety becomes an increasing problem; difficulties with authority and other unexpected complications come along. Having slogged through the difficult experiences of the past, they were not expecting these new trials to arise. Nor did they see how the damage of the past was still affecting them into adulthood.

Personal Identity

Growing out of damaged self-esteem, survivors of sexual abuse have a lot of confusion in their minds as to who they are and where they fit into this world. They want very much to be a part of the mainstream of life but are never sure just where they belong. Many of them are actually quite intelligent, capable, and talented, but they never seem to quite get their lives off the ground. They feel hindered, bound, like they are always dragging an anchor. They do things or say things they regret. Many things they try to do just don't work out. Therefore they pull back and quit taking risks. They are hesitant to express their opinion, as they have great fear of criticism or ridicule. They do not recognize their own talents. Consequently, they have difficulty reaching their full potential, simply because they have no realistic idea of their capabilities and how to put them to work. They can, therefore, become underachievers.

Many survivors don't believe anyone sees them as worthwhile persons. "After all," the survivor muses, "if I don't see anything good in me, how can anyone else possibly see anything of value." Many withdraw because of such a self-concept.

Interestingly enough, however, some go the opposite route. As a way of mentally escaping their abuse, some survivors throw themselves into their schoolwork and excel. Because they do well academically, they go further than most and may continue to forge ahead, relentlessly taking on new challenges all the time. On and on they go, reaching new heights all the time until eventually depression, anxiety, or excessive fatigue set in. At this point, their world starts to come apart, and everything so important before now begins to lose its meaning. The excitement of gaining new heights and goals crumbles to a sense of nothingness. Life seems a waste. The glamorous superstructure of their lives proves too much for the weak foundation of self, and the threat of collapse is imminent. The past has caught up with the present, and the future looks even darker.

Jill shared with me a dream in which she looked into a trash can on the curb and saw a doll, tattered and worn, with part of one leg missing. At first the dream made no sense. Later she realized the doll represented her life. She viewed herself as damaged, tattered, worn, worthless, of no use to anyone, a piece of trash to be discarded. No wonder she struggled with the question of what she was good for in this life, where she fit in, and what value she could be to anyone. Her sense of self-worth needed a lot of help.

Because of past abuse, Marjorie was convinced that she was dumb, stupid, ugly, and hateful and that she really had no life ahead of her. During her late teens, Marjorie's mother continued to reinforce those thoughts. The mother did not allow her to go out with her friends. She convinced Marjorie that no one would want her to be with them. Although Marjorie had artistic talent, her mother said her work was worthless. When Marjorie's entry won first place in the school art exhibit, her mother commented, "That was a mistake."

Being at the top of her class did not seem to mean anything to Marjorie either. As we worked through a number of her issues in therapy, especially that of her self-worth as a person, Marjorie began to slowly realize that possibly she was a worthwhile person after all, and she began to set her goals higher. With a strong interest in helping children, she went away to college and then on to medical school with the goal of becoming a pediatrician. An important corner was turned; the confusion was fading; her identity as a person was blossoming.

Gender Identity

Adult survivors of abuse experience growing feelings of doubt about their own identity as males or females. This is especially true when the abuser is the same sex as the victim. The problem is particularly prevalent with male survivors. Every male survivor I have ever worked with in therapy has tremendous doubts about his own masculinity. Please do not jump to conclusions. By no means does this mean that every male who has been sexually abused by a male is automatically homosexual or soon will be. Nothing could be further from the truth. Only a limited number who have been abused become homosexual.

Most male survivors have persistent doubts about whether they are fully masculine and can handle the demands and requirements of male roles in life. Many are not highly aggressive and tend to be more quiet and retiring. They try to avoid conflict, avoid competitive sports, shy away from macho activities, and seek individually oriented activities. They generally avoid leadership positions even when quite capable, preferring to avoid possible conflict, confrontations, and potentially threatening situations. They tend to let others make decisions for them rather than express their own preferences. They may find themselves more interested in academic pursuits, technology, or aesthetic interests such as art and music.

Joe was never sure of his masculinity. All the confidence he had mustered to succeed in high school seemed to be slowly crumbling. Doubts about his ability to take charge of his own life continued to grow. He became dependent on others to help him move forward and make decisions. Because of his uncertainty, Joe chose other males to model his life after. That helped, but he sometimes copied his models so much that he lost touch with his own personal identity. He worried a lot about how other males viewed him, fearing a repetition of the criticism and rejection of his younger years.

Because Joe did not feel confident as a male, he found himself drifting toward relationships with aggressive people who were able to be decisive and take charge of situations. He then felt relieved of pressure to take full responsibility for his life, because he now had someone he thought was wiser and more able to tell him what to do. As time went on, however, he found out these very same people he had looked up to for leadership were not necessarily wiser or more able to handle life. They were just more opinionated and impulsive,

often making poor decisions and exhibiting attitudes
and actions that hurt Joe in the process. As these relationships became hurtful, like the abuse of the past,
Joe turned inward again and tried to make it on his own.
Occasionally he would find someone who was supportive and encouraging, and he came to value those relationships very much. But such helpful people were all
too few.

Depression

Perhaps the most common problem experienced by adult
survivors of sexual abuse is that of chronic depression. Basic
symptoms of depression include some of the following:

feeling sad, hopeless, discouraged, or "down in the
   dumps"
increased irritability
loss of interest in or enjoyment of pleasurable activities
significant reduction from previous levels of sexual interest or desire
loss of appetite or increased appetite
insomnia or excessive sleep
extreme agitation or slowing down of movements and responses
decreased energy, tiredness, or fatigue
sense of worthlessness, guilt, or self-blame
difficulty thinking, concentrating, or making decisions
easily distracted
memory loss
recurrent thoughts of death or suicide[1]

Survivors of childhood sexual abuse will identify with
most of these, particularly with feelings of sadness, dejec-
tion, and hopelessness. Many have few happy days and a
generally bleak outlook on life. They take a more negative
view of life and don't expect many positive things to hap-

pen. Life is a daily struggle just to keep going, and it frequently becomes overwhelming. There always seems to be some catastrophe around the corner. Sometimes there just seems to be no strength to go on. Many days are filled with heaviness and sadness, when the tears seem to come from nowhere. The depression can come and go for no apparent reason, but it never seems to disappear completely. Something is wrong, but what?

Different survivors of abuse deal with various levels of depression, but all experience it to some extent. Some have periods of hopelessness, but they are able to get going again. For others the depression becomes unbearable, overwhelming, and continual. For those whose struggle is very severe or who are emotionally more fragile, the battle seems so hopeless and endless that they may attempt suicide as an escape from their suffering.

The deep sense of hopelessness that characterizes depression is caused by the long experience of being trapped in an abusive situation with no way out. The child could not fight off the abuser or stop the abuse. There was no way to express all the horrible feelings that built up within. Everything was trapped inside, and it became very overwhelming. The child's defeated, trapped mindset carried over into adult life. The turmoil was too great, the pain too deep; the normal growth in self-confidence and problem solving had been thwarted. The adult is stuck.

When I first met Sally, she looked tired, her face was drawn, signs of fatigue were evident. She shared her story of continual sexual abuse from the time she was a very young girl until late teens when she was finally able to get out of her virtual prison of horrors. Every word was full of pain and anguish. She spoke in hushed tones, almost a whisper that I could barely hear. She was doubled over and crumpled in her chair, her face to the floor. She found it hard to cry, for she was afraid that if she started, she would never be able to stop.

For Sally, every day was a serious struggle. She was very weary of living and was just barely making it from day to day. The pain was so great that she really wanted to die, but as a strongly committed Christian she knew that suicide would not be right in the eyes of God. She was desperate for help. Would God be angry with her for not having enough faith to go on? She firmly believed that her family would be better off without her, that she was a drag to all of them. She prayed that God would take her life, but God didn't answer. Didn't God really care that she suffered so? In the midst of her hopelessness, she somehow found enough strength to take one day at a time and keep on going.

Repressed Anger

Every survivor of sexual abuse struggles with a deep well of anger. Most have it covered and under firm control. They have carried the anger for years but often are not even aware of it, nor do they understand where it comes from. Most survivors are emotionally constricted, not letting any emotions show and working especially hard to keep anger under the surface. The presence of anger creates growing anxiety, so situations that might bring out anger are avoided at all costs.

Sue Blume points out that survivors of sexual abuse have spent all their energies dissociating from their anger, stuffing it down, and distracting themselves from it. They so disown their own anger that they are not aware of it even when expression of anger would be appropriate. They do not act angry because they never *are* really angry. In the midst of disrespect, abuse, or anything unpleasant, they will never say they are angry but only shrug it off as no big deal.[2]

Sometimes survivors of abuse act out the anger that they feel. They may become very loud, demanding, short-tempered, unstable, or even abusive as they act what they feel. The true focus of their anger may be widely diffused and well rationalized. Sometimes they will call it "righteous indignation." They believe they have every right to be angry and abusive because the other person "made me do it."

Susan was unhappy with her life. In the past she had been a quiet and submissive wife who did everything to make her husband happy because she loved him. He was an easygoing guy who was happy to let her do many things because she was very capable and talented. This gave him more time to relax and do the things he wanted.

Eventually, however, Susan's helpful and cooperative ways changed. She got tired of doing everything while her husband relaxed. She became more like a volcano, spewing her fire and brimstone everywhere. She yelled at her husband for being lazy and passive. She put him down at every turn. Nothing he could do was good enough. She got upset over small things and picked away at whatever he did. Nothing could calm her down. She had come to hate men—a feeling that actually resulted from her own childhood sexual abuse.

As I think back on some of the long-term results of my own abuse, I don't recall getting angry about much of anything. I was a stable person. Some of my friends told me that I had a smoldering personality, but they never really explained what that meant. I didn't think much about it. I did notice that some people reacted negatively to me, but I never understood why. I thought they were just being nasty—like those who had been abusive. One day while looking at class pictures from school, I saw for the first time the anger in my facial expression. There it was, plain as the nose on my face. Why hadn't I seen this before?

While in therapy I had a significant dream. I was talking with some former friends and fellow workers. Nearby were holes in the ground that glowed bright red, just like small volcanoes, threatening to erupt. The meaning of

ANGER HAS ITS ROOTS IN THE SOIL OF UNRESOLVED LOSS !!!

the dream was clear. My anger was bubbling deep within, threatening to spew out a boiling rage that could hurt anyone around. The lid could no longer stay shut. I had to face the long-repressed anger toward my abuser that had been bubbling inside all these years. I had to find ways to let the anger out, but avoid hurting others in the process.

Connecting the anger to its origin helped me understand why it was there. Finding appropriate ways to express anger without hurting anyone greatly relieved the pressure that had been there so long. Depression (frequently from anger turned inward) that had plagued me for years now faded into the background. A lot of negative thinking changed to a much more positive and upbeat lifestyle.

Anxiety

The dictionary definition of anxiety reads: "A painful or apprehensive uneasiness of mind, usually over an impending or anticipated ill. An abnormal and overwhelming sense of apprehension and fear often marked by physiological signs (as sweating, tension, and increased pulse), by doubt concerning the reality and nature of the threat, and by self-doubt about one's capacity to cope with it."[3] A working definition is that anxiety is *unconscious fear*. I am afraid of something, some impending disaster, but I don't know the real focus of the fear.

The effect of anxiety on the body is the same as the effect of fear in a real emergency. If you are driving down the highway and see an oncoming car veer into your lane, everything in your body suddenly gears up to meet the impending danger. Your blood pressure suddenly rises to send more blood and energy to the brain; split-second decisions are made; your adrenalin flows rapidly to give you the extra strength you need; your breathing becomes rapid; your muscles tense. When you narrowly avoid the impending accident, you breathe a sigh of relief. You feel like pulling over to give yourself time to relax and let your whole system calm down to normal. The crisis is past.

Anxiety has similar effects. Whenever the survivor of abuse senses a threatening situation, his or her anxiety level will immediately rise, tension will take over, the whole system will gear up for some impending catastrophe. The survivor then needs to retreat to calm down, as the anxiety can be overwhelming. Outsiders may feel this is a huge overreaction. What they do not understand is that some unconscious memories from the survivor's past abuse have been stirred up. This may take place on an unconscious level, and the survivor of abuse may not be able to explain his or her actions, but in fact some real terror of the past has been awakened and now threatens to overwhelm the survivor.

Jill didn't know what was happening to her. She had suffered with chronic depression for years. She had even been to other counselors but had not found relief. As we worked together to get at the real problem, Jill noted that when we got anywhere near certain topics, her anxiety level automatically shot up. Since she was having problems in her marriage, we were discussing her response to her husband sexually. Immediate panic set in and her anxiety level skyrocketed. The mere passing mention of the word *sex* sent her anxiety level off the charts. Somewhere she was connecting something terrifying from her past of which she had no conscious awareness.

The real problem was not in Jill's marriage relationship, for her husband was indeed a kind and gentle person who had no intention of hurting her. It took many months of therapy to even begin to recall any connecting events that made sense. Eventually memories began to surface about her father from when she was very young. At first she rejected such thoughts, even fought them off, for in her conscious memories she had looked up to her father and thought a great deal of him. But as her recall ability returned bit by bit, the evidence mounted until it became undeniable. In much anguish and tears, Jill began to acknowledge that her father had indeed violated her, not once, but many times in horrifying and terrorizing experiences when she was very young. Her conscious mind had completely blocked it out for years because it was so terrible. The anxiety gave clues to the long-buried memory. The whole nightmare was still very real and alive deep within her unconscious.

Repressed Feelings

Because of the intensity of the feelings of overwhelming fear, guilt, shame, anger, confusion, and pain experienced through the course of childhood sexual abuse, many survivors have learned to repress their feelings, pushing them into the unconscious so that they feel little of anything. Their survival technique is to go numb. Just as the survivor has the ability to repress memory of traumatic events, he or she has the ability to repress the feelings that went with the abuse. Many become so adept at it that they are not even consciously aware of shutting off what they feel. When some survivors talk about the facts of what happened, it may sound like yesterday's newspaper. There is no accompanying emotion with the account of difficult events. It is totally flat and expressionless.

The repression of feelings then carries over into adult life, where the survivor has real difficulty expressing feelings about anything in the present as well. The survivor does not seem to get very down about things that go wrong, but neither does the person get excited about things that go right. Everything is like a dull gray blob. Serious efforts to get at repressed feelings take time but are well worth the effort. Feeling alive with emotion, even though not all is positive, is certainly to be preferred to feeling half dead most of the time.

Matt knew there was sexual abuse in his background, but he had gotten along fairly well in his life until the past year or two when many things seemed to go wrong. As he tried to describe what was happening in his life, his thoughts and ideas were rather jumbled and confusing. Certain thoughts seemed to get stuck in his mind and were hard to get past. Efforts to get at feelings connected with his abuse in the past or complications in the present brought nothing at all. Matt was quite unable to get in touch with them. He realized that he felt numb inside—devoid of all identifiable feeling.

As Matt continued to work at finding the feelings part of himself, bits and pieces came through. Finally he was able to break down a lot of the walls of repression and find a host of inner feelings connected with his abuse as well as with situations in the present. At first he felt overwhelmed and fearful at finding himself in uncharted waters. But he gradually learned to balance his feelings and use them in constructive ways. He began to feel freer as a person; the jumbled thoughts straightened out; he was able to find increased stability in his life.

Guilt and Shame

The same problems of guilt and shame that begin in earlier years continue on into adulthood. All survivors of sexual abuse I have ever known continue to struggle with both of these feelings deep inside. They feel guilt for a lot of things in life, many times inappropriate and exaggerated guilt, but they do not understand the connection of these feelings to their past abuse. Along with their very strong sense of unworthiness is the deeply ingrained belief that they are evil, sinful, and not good enough for anyone to love. They may be suspicious of anyone who tries to show caring and will pull away, believing they don't deserve anyone's sincere concern.

Survivors of abuse feel as they do because they cannot understand their own actions. Since the abuse happened again and again, they believe they should have somehow stopped it; they should have been stronger, even though some were beaten or forced into submission. The sense of guilt is especially strong when, rather than being forced, they were carefully manipulated and persuaded, one seductive step at a time, and found themselves returning again and again as if under a hypnotic spell. "How could I have done this?" the survivor asks.

Only as survivors are able to picture another child the same age in the same overwhelming scenario can they begin to piece together the degree of control the abuser had over their emotions and physical responses that brought them to the point of helpless surrender. It is then that they can begin to challenge their own guilt feelings as being inappropriate.

Even more frightful than guilt is the fear of embarrassment and shame, with the subsequent sense of humiliation should others find out. The survivor expects to be automatically rejected and condemned by others, because no one can really understand his or her plight. As Hunter points out, people who feel a lot of shame will be very lonely.[4]

Because of the constant load of deep guilt and the fear of shame and humiliation, survivors often develop a neurotic lifestyle in which they may throw their energies into helping others. They may give and give of themselves to others, striving for perfection and accomplishment, hoping someone will notice and accept them as persons. They become givers because they do not feel worthy to receive, and they tend to get hooked up with takers—self-centered people who think the world revolves around them and who are glad to take anything you are willing to give them that suits their needs. Because the givers know little of helping themselves, they eventually run out of energy, and they often lose their personal identity in the process. With this self-defeating lifestyle, their energies are exhausted and collapse becomes imminent.

Sam felt guilty most of his adult life. If someone else was upset, he believed that he must have done something to cause it. If he greeted someone and that person did not answer, Sam believed that somehow he must have said something to upset the person. If something went wrong on the job, he must have caused it somehow.

The fact that he worked hard while others were goofing off did not occur to Sam to be a problem. He was bothered when others piled work on him when he was already overloaded, but he felt it was his obligation to do it all to perfection. The word *no* was not in his vocabulary. If he did get upset about the unfair burdens placed upon him, Sam felt guilt for that also. The sense of obligation drove him on and on. If a job needed doing, he stepped in and did it because he saw it as his responsibility. He would feel guilty for not doing what was needed, even though others did not carry their share.

Sam had a desperate need to be liked by his peers and authority figures, although he did not find that need fulfilled very often. He tried to do things for people, always going the second mile in everything. He tried to be the best in order to be recognized and liked by others, not because of pride, but because he wanted to escape that dreaded fear of shame and humiliation. Many times Sam was taken advantage of in his efforts, but he was willing to pay the price in order to be accepted. No one must know his inner self. That would be too dangerous.

Spiritual Confusion

Survivors of sexual abuse have some serious problems with their view of God. Even when they know intellectually what God is like, their inner feelings tell them something different. Their feelings are very confused.

Survivors know in their heads that God is love. But what is love, and how do we learn about love? Most people from reasonably normal backgrounds understand love, for they have firsthand experience growing up with caring parents and family. They understand a warm hug; they value encouragement and praise; they know how to give and receive; they know how to be emotionally close. Survivors of abuse know none of these experiences. Their lives have been devoid of genuine love and caring throughout their growing-up years. When they do finally seem to find someone who cares, that person manipulates and misuses them. Their experience teaches that caring and abuse are always linked together. Therefore, because our view of God is influenced by our earthly experience, the ability of abused persons to relate to a God of love is greatly hampered. In fact, if a child is abused by his or her father, the whole concept of father, whether earthly or heavenly, becomes very twisted and even terrifying.

How do survivors of abuse accept the concept that God will deliver them from all their troubles, when God apparently allowed all of the horrendous abuse to happen? How can survivors believe that the love of God is near, when the biological father or stepfather's nearness meant impending abuse? For survivors, closeness has become dangerous.

Many survivors of abuse are very turned off by study of Scripture, prayer, or worship of God. Talk about a closer walk with God leaves them numb. Their view of God is that he is waiting for them to mess up so he can zap them with judgment. They believe he just doesn't care how much they suffer. Their firsthand experience with the judgmental attitudes of others further reinforces their fears. What reason do they have to believe God would be any different? *Survivors of sexual abuse need to experience the spirit of acceptance, forgiveness, and caring in others before they are able to really believe it on a spiritual level.*

Jill constantly expected judgment. She was afraid to pray out loud, did not feel like studying Scripture, was often uncomfortable in church, and tended to interpret anything about God's judgment in the pastor's sermons as directly aimed at her. She loved the music of the church, but found relationships uncomfortable. Although the people of the church were friendly and seemed to accept her, she was apprehensive. Caring was confusing to her, and potentially dangerous, so she kept herself on guard.

Jill wanted to believe God really loved her, but she found it difficult to understand how a God of love could have allowed the horrible abuse she had suffered as a very young and helpless child. The experience of a father who on one hand seemed to be caring and tender with his children but at other times was nasty, evil, and hateful was too much to handle. Jill had learned not to trust her own father. How then could she trust her heavenly Father? The confusing dilemma continued for years to come.

Summary

The survivor of childhood sexual abuse has managed to scrape by the terrors of younger years and to escape his or her abuser. The hope for leaving the awful experiences behind seems to have been realized. But in adult life, too many disturbing problems keep popping up, and life never really becomes peaceful as hoped.

The old problems of self-worth continue to nip at the survivor's heels, only to be reinforced by the daily grind of life. The sense of being someone important continues to be illusive. There are only doubts, questions, and discomfort.

Depression becomes more common with its accompanying fatigue, negative thinking, and despair. Crippling anxieties become an increasing problem, so that situations the survivor could once handle now become very difficult. Certain words, smells, or situations trigger high anxiety or phobias. The survivor becomes aware of a deep underlying anger that bubbles on and on. The anger can no longer be ignored; its intensity becomes threatening. Bad memories from the past refuse to be ignored. They return in flash-backs, nightmares, or visual images.

Guilt and shame continue to destroy the survivor's self-esteem. A twisted view of God, all mixed up by the messages of abuse, further isolates the survivor. The problems of the past have become the problems of the present and the threat of the future. The survivor cries out for a different life, for deliverance, and for healing.

It is important to note that we have shifted from the term *victim* to *survivor*. The child was clearly victimized and rendered helpless. The adult, though still greatly troubled by the unresolved past, is not still a victim but rather one who learned in some way to cope with all painful things that came along. The adult has thus survived. The adult may be stuck in survival skills and may not yet know a lot about normal living, but he or she has nonetheless learned to survive.

6

Later Effects in Adult Life

Relationships

Do not fret because of evil men
or be envious of those who do wrong;
for like the grass they will soon wither,
like green plants they will soon die away.
Trust in the LORD and do good;
dwell in the land and enjoy safe pasture.
Delight yourself in the LORD
and he will give you the desires of your heart.
Commit your way to the LORD;
trust in him and he will do this:
He will make your righteousness shine like dawn,
the justice of your cause like the noonday sun.
Be still before the LORD and wait patiently for him;
do not fret when men succeed in their ways,
when they carry out their wicked schemes.
Refrain from anger and turn from wrath;
do not fret—it leads only to evil.
For evil men will be cut off,
but those who hope in the LORD will inherit the land.
A little while, and the wicked will be no more;
though you look for them, they will not be found.
But the meek will inherit the land
and enjoy great peace.
The wicked plot against the righteous
and gnash their teeth at them;
but the Lord laughs at the wicked,
for he knows their day is coming.

Psalm 37:1–13

The survivor of sexual abuse may have thought that the abuse of the past affected him or her only on an individual level. It may come as a surprise to find that the long-range effects of the abuse go much further, influencing the way the survivor relates to others—peers, authorities, and people with whom he or she works or socializes. In addition, the survivor may find it difficult to build and maintain a good marriage. A healthy marriage requires closeness, openness, and vulnerability to one's spouse—areas in which the survivor has difficulty. Each of these problem areas hinders the survivor in finding a meaningful life in the years to follow. Let us look at it in two parts: social difficulties and marriage difficulties.

Social Difficulties

Privacy Needs

Most survivors of sexual abuse need a lot of personal privacy. They do not share much of their inner feelings. Rather, they feel a high level of social discomfort and often avoid social interaction. Their strong need for privacy springs from a variety of things. They feel inferior to others, always comparing themselves to others in a negative way. They have difficulty accepting compliments, believing instead that people just say things to be kind. Their view of self is very poor, and because they do not like themselves, they do not believe that anyone else can either. They maintain a high defensive wall that practically no one can penetrate. The childhood feelings of being different from others and set apart continue into adulthood.

Eventually survivors discover that way down deep they have a very vulnerable spot and they believe they will be defenseless and hurt again if anyone ever finds it. Because they have been unable to defend themselves against the attacks and clever manipulations of their abusers in the past, and because they have been deeply hurt by those same individuals, they expect to be hurt again by others. They have an intense fear of any sort of abuse, manipulation, or being taken advantage of again. They also fear the pain of abandonment and rejection if they should venture out in relationships. They operate on the motto: "If you don't get close, you don't get hurt."

> Sam wanted to be a part of the mainstream of life just as much as anyone, but many things bothered him that he did not understand. He found himself avoiding social activities and interaction with other people. He stayed to himself a lot, didn't join in any sports, and mostly stayed at home, reading his books, puttering around the house, and listening to music. He didn't like to be out in crowds, so he avoided malls, restaurants, and other public places.
>
> Sam didn't really have friends. He preferred to be alone with his thoughts; it was more comfortable that way. Others never really knew how to relate to him. The more he avoided others, the more lonely he became. But Sam felt safer this way, and thus the loneliness became the lesser of the two problems.

The Victim Image

Although the abuse took place many years ago when the child was overpowered by someone much bigger and much more clever, the feelings of helplessness persist into adult life. Even though the survivor has plowed through many difficult situations in life, the old feeling of powerlessness keeps coming back again and again.

During the course of abuse, the child's will, desires, and sense of effectiveness as a person are continually violated. From this, a basic sense of powerlessness forms as the child's territory and space are repeatedly violated. The sense of powerlessness is further reinforced when the child's attempt to halt the abuse is frustrated. It is further increased as the child is unable to make adults understand or believe what is happening. Force and threat further increase the powerlessness.[1] As the child progresses into adulthood with a sense of powerlessness, he or she tends to remain a dependent child looking for someone to be a caretaker and feeling quite unable to care for self.

Many survivors are not sure what is normal, and do not have the skills or the initiative to care for themselves in an adult world. These adult survivors therefore remain helpless and dependent, prime targets to be taken advantage of in adult life as well.

When an exploiter senses weakness in someone, his or her instincts take over. The exploiter is attracted like a magnet to dependent, giving people. At first the exploiter is charming, friendly, and apparently a desirable person, befriending the survivor of abuse and doing everything possible to be helpful. As time goes on, however, the exploiter demands more and more from the survivor, using guilt as a weapon. When the victim seems reluctant to do what the exploiter asks, he or she simply turns on more pressure and persuasion, until the survivor gives in to the demands.

While the appropriate response would be to send the self-centered, manipulative exploiter out of his or her life, the survivor of abuse tends to become more helpless, regressing further into a childlike state, leaving himself or herself at the mercy of the exploiter. The inner child may be whining and complaining but feels powerless to take any definitive action. Thus the old feelings of victimization again take over. Even when there are many options the survivor could take to conquer his or her problem in the present, the survivor tends to retreat and not take appropriate action.

Although Janice was a quiet person, she tried to do her best at whatever task she tackled. She always did more than expected at her job, but the harder she worked, the more things seemed to pile on her. Janice never thought it was fair that others left at quitting time, but she was still piled high with extra last-minute work. Others seemed to have time to chat around the water cooler or stay longer at coffee breaks, but Janice was still plugging away. When a coworker asked Janice to do him a favor, she always tried to comply even though it was not her responsibility. She would fume within that others got away with shortcuts, and seemed to have free time, but she didn't. She really felt like telling her boss a thing or two, but never quite got around to it.

Janice complained about all the work she had to do, but nothing seemed to change. When she did finally crank up the courage to say something, it came out all wrong, as an overreaction. She felt guilty, withdrew, and went back to her pile of work, helplessly resigned to her plight. When others continued to pile their work on her, Janice tried to refuse, but never with any firmness. Others just laughed and said she needed to be more organized. When she finally got up the courage to ask her boss for a raise for all the work she was doing, he refused, saying she was just complaining, and that they would talk about it another time.

Janice felt trapped, used, and taken advantage of once more. Sinking into further despair and discouragement, she kept on trying to do a good job hoping others would notice her efforts, but nothing changed. The anger burned on, but she never did anything about it. She was too compliant and so anxious to please others that she was willing to take whatever others dished out. She didn't know what to do to change her situation.

Control

Survivors of sexual abuse are very aware of control issues in relationships. They are uncomfortable around most people, but especially around people who have a need to control others. Whenever survivors get around manipulative people who use others for their own ends, all kinds of alarm bells go off within, mistrust rises, anxiety goes up, the defensive walls go higher, and the survivor retreats to a safer

emotional distance. The casual observer will not understand the sudden reaction.

The survivor of abuse has tremendous fear of anyone
subjecting him or her to abuse again. At the sign of possible
danger, the inner child panics and retreats in terror. However, this retreat is usually emotional rather than physical.
The survivor emotionally regresses to a scared child and
wants to flee for safety. Whether the survivor understands
the dynamics of what is happening or not, the amount of
inner discomfort will cause him or her to withdraw, to
avoid the situations whenever possible. Fear takes over; old
memories have been stirred; the system is on full alert.

You may ask, "But why do survivors not stand up to people who may try to walk on them? Why not just exercise
their prerogative to refuse whatever the manipulative person is asking or trying to do?" The survivor remembers the
awful feeling of powerlessness, humiliation, and helplessness of the past abuse. He or she has learned to deal with
life by withdrawing emotionally to minimize the hurt; it is
the only escape the survivor knows. The survivor does not
yet see himself or herself as relating adult to adult but is
caught in the helpless child to powerful parent role. Therefore, it is impossible to even think of asserting himself or
herself to solve the problem.

Even though the survivor of abuse may relate to very few
people well, there will be some with whom he or she feels
comfortable. Usually these will be supportive, encouraging,
and nonjudgmental people, but even these relationships will
be limited by defensiveness and protection of the inner self.

If a survivor of abuse is forced to relate to a manipulative
or controlling person, such as in a work situation, a great
deal of stress follows. The survivor will batten down the
hatches to ride out the impending storm, if possible, but will
go through a great deal of internal suffering in the process.
The survivor will withdraw more than usual, will have little
to say about anything, will be in a constant state of tension,

and will suffer a lot of inner pain. The survivor will keep a low profile—just do the work and get out as soon as possible.

Even though survivors have battled their way through many difficult situations, they do not see themselves as strong or powerful enough to stand up to anyone. Rather than have confrontations, the survivor will absorb the wrongs and hurts. To make matters worse, the controlling person may step in and take even more control, rationalizing that no one else is getting the job done. Because controlling persons are usually rather strong willed and impulsive, they often exceed their own boundaries and step on the toes of others. At the same time, they lose respect for others, such as survivors of abuse, who do not stand up for themselves or do not set clear boundaries in relationships.

Some survivors learn to control their surroundings and maintain safety by becoming aggressive and scaring off other people or by keeping them off base by manipulation. In such cases, the controlling survivor may be just as scared inside as the withdrawn survivor, but neither knows what the other is thinking, and neither is going to blow his or her cover.

As the survivor absorbs more and more hurt and anxiety, the pressure of repressed anger builds. The survivor finally explodes. A few perceptive people who have seen what is going on all along may be silently cheering at this point, but most will wonder what in the world went wrong, for the anger seems so out of character for the survivor. The survivor may then feel guilty about his or her anger and sink back into the former passive pattern again. The pressure starts to build again, another explosion follows, and real enmity can develop. Unless something is done to resolve the situation, it may cause hard feelings that could lead to a permanent rift in the relationship.

Problems with Authority

Similar to the dynamics between the survivor and controlling people is the problem of the survivor with authority figures. A person in authority has automatic power and control simply because of his or her position. If the authority figure is an aggressive, intimidating person, the survivor of abuse may have serious problems to contend with. A re-enactment of the parent-child relationship quickly forms, and the survivor is again on the defense.

In a work situation, the survivor will usually try very hard to please his or her supervisor but at the same time may be suffering inside. The supervisor will tend to view the quiet, somewhat timid employee as inadequate, in need of a push, and as a result come off as critical and demeaning. The survivor will feel the heat. Old messages of danger, helplessness, fear, confusion, and buried anger will boil up from within. The survivor may work to the point of exhaustion, trying to get some recognition of what he or she can do so that the boss will lighten up. But because the survivor does not say much, the hard work tends to go unnoticed. As the aggressive supervisor pours on more pressure, the survivor struggles to just survive. As the survivor's inner pressure becomes intense, explosions may occur. Because the survivor of abuse is able to absorb more pain than most, he or she will continue on in the unhappy situation, be passed over for promotions, crank out the work, and just endure. But the joy of life is gone.

A different kind of supervisor, however, will bring out an entirely different kind of response. A warm, supportive authority will generally bring out the best in the survivor of abuse and will gain the utmost in respect, loyalty, and productivity.

> Joe was having a strong inner battle concerning some of his fellow workers. Some did not seem to treat him fairly. They put him down, belittled him, cast doubt on his abilities, and undermined his accomplishments. Joe recognized insincerity in these same people. They lacked integrity in their dealings with others, playing favorites and telling people what they wanted to hear rather than giving

honest opinions. They seemed to have a need for power and control, manipulating and using others to get what they wanted for themselves.

Joe could see a lot of this going on but he was unsure what to do about it. He avoided these people when possible, but as he was forced to work in closer relationships with them, he found his own life becoming increasingly uncomfortable. He became more guarded about his opinions and thoughts, but becoming an even more private person seemed to strain the relationships even more. What to do?

To make matters worse, Joe's boss was a demanding, critical, negative, controlling person as well, who seemed to expect a great deal. Nothing Joe did seemed to be satisfactory, and the boss was always finding something about which to yell at him. Joe was feeling tremendous pressure; he had a strong need to have his boss happy with him, to have better rapport with fellow workers, and to be at peace with himself. A tall order. When would it ever end? Joe was miserable.

Joe struggled with the problem for as long as he could and finally left that job to move on to other employment. But he never felt right about not having resolved the situation he left. The memories followed him for some time. He seemed to respond to honest, supportive, encouraging authority figures well enough, but critical, aggressive ones were too much for him. He finally realized that he couldn't avoid them all, and he needed to learn how to relate to all types of authority.

Marriage Difficulties

Phyllis was so happy to be able to marry Charles, the young man she had admired all through high school. He was such a gentleman; he treated her kindly, brought her flowers, showed all the little niceties that win the heart of a young lady. "Surely he loves me very deeply," she thought. She was anxious to get out of her parents' home and to escape her stepfather and his sexual abuse. Although his abuse had stopped, he still treated her poorly, she was afraid of him, and relations remained strained. Her new fiancé seemed capable of taking care of so many situations and was handy at so many things. Charles seemed so concerned about the problems in her home and wanted to get her out of that situation.

The fact that Charles demanded sex before marriage did not bother Phyllis, since she really loved him and didn't want to lose him. The marriage seemed to get off to a good start, and they began a family. Phyllis believed she had finally found her dream of a good relationship. As time went on, however, Phyllis was somewhat bothered that Charles did not want to discuss very much with her. Whenever a problem arose, he told her the "right way" to do it, insisted there was no other way to get the job done, and refused to listen to any other ideas. When there was a real difference of opinion, he always somehow convinced her she was wrong and his way was best.

Phyllis noted that Charles became rather harsh with their children. After one heartrending episode, Phyllis strongly objected to the way he was correcting their daughter. Charles became enraged and hit her. Phyllis was flabbergasted! What happened? What did she do to deserve this? She tried to discuss what had happened, but Charles only became enraged again, accusing her of getting him upset and creating problems when he knew what he was doing all along. Something within Phyllis retreated. She sealed off the incident and tried to move on.

Phyllis was not happy with the way things were going. Any time she tried to talk about their problems, Charles refused to admit there were any. He claimed the problems were all hers, and if she didn't get herself straightened out, things would be even worse. Her husband became more threatening, and the abuse scene was often repeated. Phyllis realized she could not continue to subject herself or her children to this increasingly frightening situation. One evening after Charles had badly beaten her, she decided this was enough. She got a restraining order to keep him out of the house and began divorce proceedings.

A few years later, Phyllis met George at a social event. He seemed very nice. She was immediately attracted to him but was careful to take the relationship slowly. George didn't seem to mind and he did not push her very hard for sexual involvement as Charles had. George seemed very thoughtful of her, was especially kind to the children, and they responded well to him. The children even asked their mother when George was going to become their new father. He seemed to be very concerned about their financial struggles as a single-parent family and even helped them out on several occasions. George had proven himself to be dependable, sensitive to her needs, and very good to the children.

Phyllis finally decided marriage was right for her and that George was the one. They began their new life together. George seemed like a wonderful man and he continued to take a great interest in her children. He helped out in getting them ready for bed, giving them their baths, reading stories, and showing them affection. Phyllis had a good sex life with her new husband. They seemed to be able to communicate well and they had few conflicts. Phyllis thought she finally had made it.

As time went on, Phyllis noted a few times that her daughter had some red, inflamed areas around her vagina, but she didn't think too seriously about it. A couple of times Phyllis found blood stains in her daughter's panties, but again she did not give it serious thought. But when it continued to happen, Phyllis took her daughter to a doctor to determine what sort of disorder might be causing the problem. The doctor examined the girl carefully and then began to ask Phyllis some serious questions about the bleeding as well as the red marks in the vaginal area. The doctor then frankly told Phyllis that her daughter was being sexually molested and that she must put a stop to it immediately. He explained that it was his duty by law to report the incident to the authorities and that she could expect an investigation by the child welfare authorities.

Phyllis was in a state of shock! How could this be happening to her daughter? How, who, when, how long had it been going on? Why hadn't she had any clues? Why didn't her own daughter tell her? But as her mind flashed back to her own abuse, she understood her daughter's fear and consequent silence. In a rage she confronted her husband. Initially George denied it but finally admitted he had "lost control a time or two." Phyllis was brokenhearted. She could never trust another man again.

The authorities came and made their investigation. Phyllis watched her husband go to jail. She knew the marriage could not continue. She had to somehow pick up the pieces of her life and go on.

Without realizing it, Phyllis had unconsciously married someone just like her stepfather. She had remained a victim—a helpless, dependent child. Because she never did anything about her own problem, the same fate had come to her daughter. Now was the time to stop the whole self-perpetuating process for both her and her daughter. She found a counselor who understood her needs, and both she and her daughter began their journey back to health and normalcy.

In no other area of life are the long-lasting effects of childhood sexual abuse more prominent than in marriage. No other human relationship requires as much openness and honesty, problem-solving ability, mutual nurturing, or emotional closeness. None of these skills are found in the background of the survivor. Instead of openness, the survivor has learned to be on guard, to avoid letting anyone get very close. The survivor has learned to keep his or her emotions under control. The old defenses against hurt actually serve to undermine the marriage bond, eventually threatening destruction of the relationship. Let's look at some of the important issues.

Attraction Issues

Some survivors have become determined that no one, absolutely no one will ever victimize them again. Therefore, in choosing a marriage partner, the survivor chooses someone with whom he or she feels comfortable. Although the underlying reasons for the attraction to a potential partner may not have been given that much thought, the comfort zone will include the sense of safety, security, respect, and a nonabusive, predictable relationship.

The basic interaction between husband and wife will go along fine for some time, but marital strain starts to develop. The survivor begins to view the spouse as dull, uninteresting, very predictable, lacking spontaneity, and just plain boring. The spouse seems so passive and easygoing, never getting excited about anything. Is there really life inside?

Because the spouse is so easygoing and nonthreatening, problems do not get resolved, needed jobs and errands aren't done. Neither partner really wants to have to hash out a difficulty; neither likes confrontation. Therefore, unresolved problems build and build until they eventually become mountains of mammoth proportions. The marriage drifts like a ship with no rudder, and the closeness that was once there slowly dies. The survivor of abuse may take charge of the situation so that important things in life do get done, but he or she resents winding up with most of the responsibility and may sound off about it from time to time, but with no measurable effect. The survivor begins to feel increasingly insecure in the relationship, questioning if his or her spouse would really be there to help in time of crisis.

Other survivors of abuse may still be stuck in the child victim image, feeling very helpless to deal with life. This kind of survivor may be attracted to someone who seems to know how to take charge of things in life, who seems to know what to do and how to handle situations that require confrontation or the ability to assert oneself. Again, the marriage will go fine for a time, and then dissatisfaction sets in. The more aggressive spouse will do what he or she thinks best in handling situations that come along, and the more passive survivor will do what he or she knows best—helplessly go with the flow. Eventually one or the other becomes tired of his or her role and wants to change. The survivor may become tired of remaining like a child and want to take more of the family responsibility. Or the more dominant spouse becomes tired of carrying all the responsibility and wants a rest. Unless the two partners in marriage are willing to change their respective roles at the same time, each making new adjustments to the changes in the relationship balance, there will be considerable confusion. The old unseen rules of interaction have changed, and neither is sure what will happen next. Mutual insecurity sets in. Without professional help, the marriage may not make it.

Still others choose what is familiar, not recognizing the early warning signs. As in Phyllis's story, they unconsciously choose someone who is like their abuser because that is familiar and in some way exciting. At first the relationship seems to be ideal—with a take-charge type of person who at the same time seems to be sensitive and caring, someone whom others look up to. Only later does the survivor find out the hidden truth, that under the well-polished facade is a self-willed person who is abusive and controlling. Only as the survivor works through the pain, anger, confusion, self-blame, and excitement phases of the past abuse will he or she be able to separate emotionally from the original abuser and thus be much better prepared to have a normal and healthy relationship in marriage.

Fear of Closeness

Closeness, or emotional intimacy, becomes a major hurdle in marriage to the survivor of abuse. Although desperately hungry for someone to really care and show affection, the survivor is likewise afraid of the very thing he or she so desperately needs. Since the ability to build a close relationship begins in the experience of one's own family of origin, the survivor comes into marriage at a distinct disadvantage. Closeness and abusive or exploitive relationships, hurt, confusion, anger, fear, and pain all got mixed in together. The survivor's defensive wall of protection from further hurt may well have worked in the past, but it now blocks the quest for intimacy in marriage.

At first the problem is not apparent. Each partner is so busy with early issues in the relationship—such as getting to know each other's ways and habits, starting a home, getting established in a career, beginning a family, and walking the baby at night—that there is little time for in-depth companionship. However, as time goes on, new discoveries about each other become infrequent, the children are older and involved in school, careers are moving along, life settles down to more predictable routines. At this point the couple look more to each other for a deeper relationship. In a healthy marriage, the couple will now focus more on their relationship with each other, will take more time to share their inner thoughts and feelings, will become very attuned to the needs of each other, and will be dedicated to each other's growth and well-being.

Survivors of sexual abuse may find this stage of marriage hard to handle. For them, the formula has been: self-disclosure means weakness, weakness means vulnerability, vulnerability means exploitation, and exploitation brings deep hurt and pain. Who needs that? The walls go up.

Each of us has our own measure of emotional closeness that we consider safe. Fear of closeness is usually a mutual rather than individual problem. Clinical data supports the fact that a person who has a problem with emotional closeness usually marries someone with essentially the same level of discomfort. It is a problem they both face. But as the requirements of emotional closeness increase, soon the tolerable limits of safe distance are reached. Danger signals start going off inside the survivor, and the protective walls go up. The sense of closeness in the relationship comes to a grinding halt.

Fear of closeness can show itself in many ways in a marriage:

1. *Constant bickering.* The couple is frequently arguing about something or another, although the content of the argument does not seem to be the main problem, for it is nothing of significance. The couple never keep on the subject but go from one argument to another.

What is happening? Simply this: As long as they are arguing they are still involved with each other and want to be with each other. However, closeness is perceived as dangerous; thus the arguments serve the purpose of keeping the couple at a safe distance from each other while at the same time still attached.

2. *High achievers.* This couple is always busy with many things. They not only work many hours at job and home, but they are also very involved in church and community. They seem to be on almost every committee, helping wherever they can, deeply involved in important activities in and out of the home. Many people admire them for their dedication, their ability, and their efficiency and wish to be like them. But not everything is as it appears on the surface.

This couple may be having a problem with emotional closeness. They simply handle their need for distance by being so involved in worthwhile causes that they have little time for each other. They drop into bed late at night, too exhausted to take time to nurture each other. "We just can't seem to find the time," they complain. Only after a great struggle one or the other may give up some pet project in order to have more time for their relationship, only to take on another important duty that someone desperately needs done. The relationship doesn't deepen, remains stagnant, and eventually dies for lack of nurturing.

3. *Parent-child interaction.* This couple is busy acting out roles. One may play the role of a parent in a marriage, taking the main load of responsibility, trying to spur the other spouse to action. The other spouse acts the role of the helpless child who has to be told everything to do, or the role of a rebellious teenager who will always get to it later or will do the opposite of what is asked.

For example, the wife may ask the husband to please call if he has to work late. He not only forgets to call when he works late, but he makes other stops on his way home so that he is later than ever. The wife becomes infuriated when this happens again and again. The wife asks him to please take out the garbage, which is now overflowing its container onto the floor. He agrees, "in a minute"—and it doesn't happen. The more she nags and reminds him of things that need doing, the less he does. He resents her spoiling his fun by all the things she has for him to do. She resents him for his many broken promises and inability to do things for himself. As they harbor their mutual resentment for each other, an emotional distance is maintained, but each one keeps his or her respective place in the family structure. They can continue this way until one of the two gets tired of his or her role and wants to change it. But if the other is not ready to change, real confusion and conflict will begin.

4. *Mutual immaturity.* Sometimes a marriage may unite two very immature partners. They are basically still children in adult clothes who are self-centered, demanding what they each want, and wanting it now. They may run up debts from impulsive spending either individually or jointly. When their credit has reached its maximum, they are stuck with huge bills that they can barely pay. Or they may go out together frequently for nights on the town—neglecting their children while having a good time.

Although they may be in this together, they are not developing closeness at all, only satisfying their own immediate needs. The huge debts may hold them together, but none of this is nurturing the marriage, only straining it. Before they can even begin to think closeness, they have to first grow up, face the responsibilities of life, get their own house in order, and then work on nurturing their relationship. Marriage is for adults only.

5. *Competition for control.* In this scenario, each spouse is trying to maintain control of the situation and/or each other. Both are strong headed, determined that "no one is going to tell me what to do!" Each has a fear of being controlled, because each has the belief that it would mean weakness, vulnerability, and certain hurt.

Each spouse has personal standards that he or she expects the partner to live up to, but neither is going to budge unless the other makes the first move as proof of sincerity. Failure to make the first move is interpreted as lack of interest, and each accuses the other of not caring. The conflict will never be resolved because neither party is willing to give in, and no one realizes that the real problem is that both are afraid of emotional closeness.

6. *Silence.* Perhaps the saddest scenario of all is the couple who has very little to say to each other. The wife is always busy in the kitchen, cleaning, or with some other homemaking project besides her regular job. The husband is busy after hours with many projects in the basement, outdoors, or somewhere else. When they do sit down to a meal, they have little to say to each other. When the meal is done, the husband disappears again to his projects while the wife cleans up the dishes and kitchen. They are rarely even in the same part of the house. The same effect can be produced when both spouses are overly involved in good ministries connected with their church that gradually undermine their relationship by distance and neglect.

Closeness never has a chance to get off the ground in this

marriage. Their relationship is characterized by emptiness and loneliness. But loneliness can be more comfortable than stirring up the fears of being hurt by trying to develop more closeness.

These examples are some of the many ways that couples avoid closeness with each other. But a word of caution: Just because you see these patterns in others, or even in your own relationship, do not automatically assume that there has been child abuse. There are many other traumas and difficulties in early years that can produce similar results with accompanying fears of intimacy.

Inability to Love

The survivor has never known genuine love. Erotic stimulation coupled with exploitation, manipulation, persuasion, or force is all the survivor really knows for certain. Caring in the dysfunctional home of the survivor was usually either nonexistent or very empty and conditional on certain compliant behaviors. Many a survivor of abuse has battled through adult life with a deep ache of loneliness that never goes away. Most have been caught up in the futile effort to please others by trying hard to be what is expected, hoping to obtain some kind of love or recognition in return.

Genuine, sincere, caring, accepting, giving, sacrificing love is totally foreign and quite suspect to survivors of abuse simply because they have never experienced it. They have only known exploitation, yet they hunger for something better. Their deeply ingrained beliefs make marriage difficult. No matter how much the partner tries to show genuine caring, the survivor of abuse will hold back, wondering when the expected exploitation or abuse will take place. No amount of reassurance will make the doubts vanish. Only a long pattern of consistent caring will gradually erode the old belief system and enable the survivor to find the real love he or she seeks.

Essential to the ongoing growth of any marriage is a very deep trust for one another. No relationship can survive without trust, but it has many levels and degrees. To find the deep and genuine love in marriage that most desire requires a *total* trust and commitment to one another. The survivor of sexual abuse, repeatedly betrayed as a child by someone who was supposed to love and protect, will have serious difficulty fully trusting anyone again. Trust can be developed, but only by the long and consistent efforts of an understanding marriage partner over a number of years.

As Janice looked back over her years of marriage, she wondered how they had ever made it as a couple. She realized she had little concept of what love really was from her background. The first few years of marriage were rather rocky, with a number of conflicts, strains, and difficulties. She was usually expecting the worst, that their marriage wouldn't make it, that her husband would want to leave her. She didn't understand her husband's needs very well. She was too wrapped up in her own problems of trying to find herself in life, her own identity as a person, her own worth and value, and filling the deep and empty void within her soul.

Janice's husband was a pastor and Janice was deeply committed to Christian ministry and values. The whole idea of possible marriage failure was a scary thing. She tried very hard to please her husband by doing things she thought he would like, but she did not seem to be very successful. There was usually a problem somewhere. She gave in to him many times as an expression of her caring, but she often got criticism in return.

Janice kept most of her feelings to herself because she didn't want to be hurt. Sometimes when the frustration got too bad, she took very long walks to think and pray and find some peace. She didn't realize that her actions were being misinterpreted and were actually contributing negatively to the already existing problems. She was used to a conditional love, expecting to receive some sort of acceptance if she did the right things. No matter what she did, her husband was too wrapped up in his work to even notice her. The more that needed to be done in his ministry at the church, the more involved he became, leaving her to take care of the children herself and spend her spare time alone. She felt a lot of rejection.

Janice did find that as she was gradually able to communicate her own loneliness and need for caring, her husband was increasingly able to understand her needs and to give her more personal time. This in turn relieved her fears; she was able to trust more of herself with him, and she began to understand his method of consistent caring over time. She began to understand more of the dimensions of love that make a marriage as found in the Scriptures and sought to follow them in her own life.

> Love is patient, love is kind. It does not envy, it does not boast, it is not proud. It is not rude, it is not self-seeking, it is not easily angered, it keeps no record of wrongs. Love does not delight in evil but rejoices with the truth. It always protects, always trusts, always hopes, always perseveres. Love never fails.
> 1 Corinthians 13:4–8

The more Janice understood what *real* love was all about, and the more she was able to apply it to her own marriage, the more their relationship improved. She became a happier person as she allowed these truths to take over in her life.

Sexual Confusion and Blockage

One of the most difficult areas in marriage for survivors is the sexual relationship itself. For most people with normal backgrounds, the sexual relationship becomes one of great pleasure and enjoyment. It becomes a means of most intimate communication, of giving great pleasure to one another. The physical, emotional, and spiritual union of the two partners in a loving relationship of marriage greatly strengthens their bond of love and caring for one another.

The survivor of sexual abuse has little concept of sex as an expression of love. Sex has become dirty, morbid, painful, emotionally confusing, and frightening. Sex represents betrayal, exploitation, humiliation, shame, hurt, and a sense of powerlessness. Many survivors of sexual abuse want nothing to do with it. They see it as total lust. Some, therefore, remain single and never want to have anything to do with the opposite sex again. They might possibly be interested in a platonic relationship where sex never enters the picture, but such a relationship is hard to find.

Nevertheless most survivors do marry, and many of them start out well, seeming to have put many unhappy memories behind them. They are aware, whether conscious or not, that sex is very much a part of a marriage, no matter how tangled their previous experience had become. Some will enter into the marriage with gusto, expecting to find something far better than they had ever known before. Their sexual drive may have become strong because of early induced stimulation. Thus for a few years the marriage will seem to work out well.

As life goes on, however, some of the old memories come intruding into conscious awareness. Feelings of fear, panic, anger, or disgust come closer to the surface. The survivor of abuse may begin to identify his or her spouse with the abuser and begin resisting sex in marriage. Just the memories themselves may be sufficient to turn off the normal sexual desire, and the survivor may begin to look for reassurance that the spouse wants him or her for more than a body, putting up roadblocks to the sexual relationship. If the spouse does not understand the change and becomes more demanding or frustrated, this will only confirm to the survivor that the only thing important is his or her body, just like it was to others in the past. Unless there is open communication about what is really going on within the survivor, the marriage is headed for a lot of trouble. Major misunderstandings arise, tempers begin to flare, frustration and defeat set in.

Some survivors don't get much beyond the wedding day before trouble begins. They may be very much in love with the person they marry, but they begin to become anxious at the time of the wedding. When it comes to sex in marriage, they freeze. The unconscious fears of the past come roaring to the surface, and panic sets in. No matter how much they tell themselves on a conscious level that this is a different kind of a relationship, one of genuine love and caring, the child within is too frightened to listen to reason, and total blockage sets in. The survivor cannot go on with a normal marriage.

Still others bail out shortly before the wedding date as their anxiety level becomes overwhelming. They are unable to separate in their minds a normal marriage relationship and horrible memories of their past abuse. The prospective bride or groom is left confused, bewildered, and very hurt. Hopes and dreams are shattered.

Mary Ann, an attractive young woman working on her second marriage, presented herself in my office. Things weren't going so well, and she didn't know what to do about it. She began by bringing me up-to-date on her two marriages. Her first marriage had failed because they hadn't gotten along together. He had not treated her well, had been unfaithful to her, and finally left her for another woman. She admitted to having difficulty responding to him sexually, but initially that problem seemed to be the result of poor communication as well as his disrespect of her. The marriage ended.

After some time, Mary Ann met another man who treated her much better. After taking some time to get to know him, Mary Ann felt she was truly in love. Although somewhat against Mary Ann's standards as a committed Christian, she agreed to have sex with him a few times before marriage, and it went very well. Encouraged that everything would be all right, she entered her second marriage.

Once the relationship had moved into marriage, however, things began to change. Mary Ann became increasingly uncomfortable with their sexual relationship, and sex itself became painful. The real cause for the physical pain was anxiety and fear, which made her freeze up and block her normal response. Mary Ann tried hard to conquer her difficulty as her husband became increasingly impatient. However, her fears were too great; she could not overcome the problem. Defeated, she soon gave up and left the marriage. She felt a total failure. The emotional scars of her past abuse were too overwhelming to face and conquer.

Summary

The world of adult relationships brings unexpected problems to the survivor of childhood sexual abuse. Many old fears resurface. Relationships become a problem, for the survivor is very wary of most people, especially those who have a need to control others. To avoid being victimized again, the survivor will withdraw to avoid a potential threat. When withdrawal is not possible, the survivor may revert to a helpless state, experience a lot of stress, which may in turn escalate to the point of personal crisis.

A similar problem emerges with authority figures, where there is a built-in differential of power. The survivor will do well with authority figures who are kind, considerate, supportive, and encouraging but very poorly with those who are demanding, critical, and insensitive. Because a controlling type of authority represents potential exploitation, the survivor's anxiety, depression, and fear escalate to the point of personal crisis. Eventually the survivor may either fold under the pressure or leave the job.

Even greater relationship skills are required in marriage. Essential ingredients are openness, emotional honesty, trust, and the ability to become vulnerable to each other. The survivor feels threatened; the fear of being hurt or exploited rises to the surface. Normal expressions of caring in marriage become confused. The survivor may withdraw into the old familiar protective shell, unable to give or receive love. The spouse does not understand what is happening and usually interprets all of this as personal rejection. Love becomes tangled with exploitation and mistrust. Sex becomes extremely frightening—an expression of brutality, confusion, and lust, instead of a sharing of deep love for one another. The relationship becomes strained and confused, producing its own hurts and unhappiness. Emotional distance seems safer.

The past may be the past, but its long-lasting damage cannot be ignored. Survivors of childhood sexual abuse have many serious problems to overcome that affect every day of their adult lives for years to come both in social relationships and in marriage.

Part 3
Identifying the Abuse

7

Recognizing the Problem

If an enemy were insulting me,
  I could endure it;
if a foe were raising himself against me,
  I could hide from him.
But it is you, a man like myself,
  my companion, my close friend,
with whom I once enjoyed sweet fellowship
  as we walked with the throng to the house of God.

But I call to God
  and the LORD saves me.
Evening, morning and noon
  I cry out in distress,
  and he hears my voice.

Psalm 55:12–14, 16–17

Although many survivors know the facts of their abuse rather well, most have not connected the abuse of the past with present problems of life. Therefore, they do not get at the root of their present difficulties. A host of others have successfully blocked off their memories as a survival technique to survive the trauma. They know only that there are large gaps in their childhood memories they cannot explain. Vague but overwhelming feelings come and go, but they have few clues as to what is wrong.

In today's world where the subject of childhood sexual abuse has become a hot topic, how can a person be sure whether or not abuse actually occurred in one's childhood? Why is the information so hidden from view if indeed it did happen? What makes it seem so remote and distant? The survivor may wonder if this is a figment of his or her imagination. The following material should help us understand the answers to these questions.

Initial Symptoms

Few people show up in a therapist's office saying, "I have been sexually abused in my growing-up years, and I want to overcome its effects on my everyday life." Most of the time they come for other reasons, not recognizing connections with a confused and oppressive past they would rather forget. More frequently the presenting symptoms are such things as chronic underlying depression and/or anxiety. There are good days and bad days, but a deep, pervasive sadness remains. Depression may have been present for years. Anxiety comes and goes, but the real cause remains elusive. Among other presenting problems may be that of low self-esteem hindering progress in the person's life. Or it may be a marriage that is not working out right, or a great deal of strain in a relationship.

The majority of those who present themselves in a pastor's or therapist's office range in age from early thirties to forties. Some have rather good insight into their personal dynamics, are in touch with their thoughts and emotions, and have given careful attention to their spiritual life. But search and try as they may, their lives do not work out right. The same problems repeat themselves over and over, and real progress is not to be found.

Others come for help with absolutely no idea what is going on inside of them. They are not in touch with their feelings at all. They are adrift in most areas of their life. Some are emotionally unstable, others basically stable. Some have many memories of their developmental years, others have none at all—a total blank. Still others have large gaps in childhood memories during specific years. Few

have any real understanding of the connection of their early
childhood sexual abuse to their present difficulties.

Following a term of Christian service abroad, Jennifer
came to my office in great distress. She was having
symptoms of severe depression and a lot of inner confusion, without a clue as to the origin of her problems. At
first we probed possibilities of side effects from medicines for tropical parasites or other possible physical origins. Those avenues revealed nothing.

Since Jennifer reported huge gaps of memory from her
growing-up years, we began digging into the past. We
used journaling—the writing of thoughts and feelings on
a daily basis—and dream interpretation to get at the unconscious origins of her problem. Each week she
brought several written pages of material—emerging
memories from her past. Each session was painful, as
she began to recall far-reaching emotional abuse from
her mother and extensive sexual abuse from her brother
and his friends over a number of years.

As we worked through the memories and the feelings
locked up inside, the depression began to improve, and
the confusion began to fade. The origin of the problem
was found. After one and a half years of therapy, Jennifer
returned with her family to her overseas ministry. A follow-
up visit several years later revealed significant and long-
lasting progress.

Sandy came for an initial evaluation and questions about
her marriage of one year. She described her husband as
wonderful—on paper. He was kind, compassionate, patient, thoughtful, dependable, caring, affectionate, and
stable. She considered them to be best friends with
each other. So what was wrong? Well, she did not feel
that attracted to him sexually; the spark just wasn't
there. She had found another who turned her on and was
wondering just what to do.

Sensing a message of sadness in her eyes, I asked her later in the interview if she had ever been molested. She was a bit taken back and wanted to know why I asked. She proceeded to reveal a very dysfunctional background in which her father was an alcoholic, was physically abusive toward various members of the family, and was repeatedly sexually abusive of Sandy herself. No wonder she was having marital problems.

Sandy was attracted to her husband because he was safe and secure. She was comfortable with him; she could trust him. But the answer was not to be found in running off with someone more exciting who might well turn out to be as abusive as her father. The true solution needed to be focused on the roots of the problem that stemmed from her victimized childhood and how that impacted her present life.

Matt frequently called on the phone about one crisis after another with many problems all somehow mixed up together. His feelings were numb, and he had little insight as to what was going on. He acted impulsively, many times getting himself into jams because of poor judgment or poor self-control. When he did do something wrong, no matter how small, Matt had strong impulses to confess to others—most of the time inappropriately. People began to believe he had some serious problems.

Matt thought most of his trouble came from the fact that he had gotten his girlfriend pregnant and had insisted on her having an abortion. Not being a Christian at the time, he thought that abortion was the thing to do because he was too immature to take on the responsibilities of marriage and family. He was already aware of some sexual abuse in his background, but he did not see how it related to his present problems. He continued to go from one panicky crisis to another.

Matt had been to several therapists, some being specialists in abortion recovery, each of whom urged him to pursue therapy for his sexual abuse. As he began therapy with me, the confusion of obsessive thoughts began to unravel, and deep layers of guilt and shame began to emerge based on his own abuse as well as some abusive acts with other children. The anger and deep emotional pain began to surface, along with his own serious doubts about his masculinity. At the root of most of his problems was his own sexual abuse with the other problems branching out from there.

Although the behavior of each of these examples varied widely, they each shared something in common. Each had come from a background of childhood sexual abuse. Each was suffering in his or her present life because of a similar trauma in the past. Each had acted on the shared trauma in diverse ways, and thus their adult lives appeared on the surface to be quite different. None had connected his or her present suffering to the history of sexual abuse.

Blocks to Understanding

Why don't survivors of sexual abuse recognize the origins of their problems? Why do they go on year after year struggling against great odds, allowing themselves to be taken advantage of again and again, fighting off severe self-doubts and self-deprecation, wading through the mire of guilt and shame for things they never caused? Why can't they see the cause of their problems and get free from their bondage?

Built into every one of us is something called a *defense mechanism*. Our minds have the ability to protect us from trauma that is too difficult to handle. The mind builds a defensive wall around the wounds of life so that we are able to go on without being totally devastated. Just as the body can build a protection around a flesh wound and continue to function even though the offending foreign body still remains under the skin, so the mind has ways to erect a wall of defense against threatening intrusions into our inner self. The following are some of the more common defense mechanisms.

> *Rationalization:* The unconscious ability to justify or make consciously tolerable by reasonable means, feelings, behavior, and motives that would otherwise be intolerable. This is not the same as conscious evasion, where the person consciously chooses to sidestep unwanted issues. For example, a survivor may rationalize that since the abuser was a well-respected person in the community and was looked up to by the family, he could not have abused me in this way. I must have somehow caused it.
>
> *Denial:* The ability to resolve emotional conflict and ward off anxiety by blocking from conscious awareness certain thoughts, feelings, wishes, or needs that the person would consider undesirable or intolerable. For example, a person may consider anger as frightening and undesirable, and therefore block it, and be quite unaware of any anger within. When presented with evidences of underlying or smoldering anger, the person will adamantly deny its presence, because there is no conscious awareness of its being there.
>
> *Repression:* The ability to block from consciousness *all* negative feelings, ideas, or impulses and to keep them out of consciousness. This process is different from suppression, where a person may *consciously* suppress certain feelings or impulses and thus keep them under control. Repression is a totally *unconscious* process in that the person is not consciously aware of blocking off undesirable thoughts, feelings, and impulses. It is something like a switch in the person's head that automatically shuts off the undesirable. For example, the person may feel a lot of guilt, anger, and hurt but not even be aware of it because the feelings are so completely repressed. The individual will therefore be un-

aware of most feelings. Even positive feelings will have difficulty coming through to a conscious level.

Projection: The ability to block off that which is emotionally unacceptable to the individual, to unconsciously reject it, and to attribute or project the problem to others. The problems attributed to others are real to the individual, and the individual reacts accordingly. For example, the individual may project his or her own feelings of guilt onto others, and thus make them feel guilty.

Introjection: The unconscious ability by which a person may turn hatred or unwanted feelings within himself or herself—the opposite of *projection.* For example, a severely depressed person may take angry or hostile feelings directed toward another and turn them back upon self. Or, a person who has been taken advantage of by another may turn the anger upon self by such thoughts as, "I deserve what is happening because I am no good," or "If I were any good at all people would like me."

Displacement: The unconscious ability to transfer or displace an emotion from its original object to a more acceptable substitute. For example, a survivor may not be able to accept anger toward his or her abusive father but may be able to feel and express anger toward other males, such as a spouse or authority figures, much out of proportion to the presenting problems at the time.

Dissociation: A splitting off of the mind, or psychological separation, that happens automatically in the presence of severe trauma. Because the trauma is so great, the mind completely blocks the feelings and memory by an amnesiac barrier so that the past trauma seems to be totally separate from the person. A more familiar type of amnesia is found in the example of people who are found wandering around who have no conscious memory of who they are, where they came from, or who they are connected to. The memory loss comes as the result of a severe trauma. The memories are driven so deeply into the unconscious that it is difficult to recover the early memories to promote healing. In such cases, memories may at first appear only as fragments or flashbacks. Dissociation is the defense mechanism at work in the problem of multiple personalities, although it may show itself in other forms.[1]

There are other defense mechanisms that we could look at, but these are sufficient for our purposes.

Please note that all of the defense mechanisms listed are *unconscious*, that is, they operate quite independently of whether or not the person is consciously thinking of them, and thus the person is generally not aware of what is happening. All of the defense mechanisms serve as a protection of the inner self so that the individual is able to cope with areas of life that would otherwise be too difficult and unmanageable. The greater the trauma to the person, the more complex the defenses become, and the greater the struggle to maintain a normal life. Although the defenses were originally erected in childhood in order to survive the trauma of abuse, they continue into adult life long after the main trauma is past and affect how the survivor relates to adult life.

It then becomes the task of therapy to dig below the unconscious and get to the areas of fear, hurt, guilt, shame, self-hatred, and anger that are still well protected. The survivor is thus helped to learn how to deal with these buried issues effectively, as well as how they impact his or her present day-to-day life. As this is done, the need for a complicated defense mechanism diminishes, the survivor is able to face issues never before faced and is freed to live a normal, productive, and happy life.

Memory Gaps

A number of persons who have survived the trauma of childhood sexual abuse have large memory gaps from early years. For example, they may recall many things before the age of five and after the age of twelve, but nothing between. The survivor is very frustrated by this phenomenon. "I hear others talk about those periods in their life, things they did then, but I draw a big blank. What is wrong with my mind? I'm too embarrassed to tell anyone I don't remember."

Although the survivor may conclude that premature senility has set in, or that his or her brain is defective, such is not the case. Once the process of defense mechanisms is understood, we can comprehend that the mind has simply blocked the conscious memory of terrible things that were happening back then for the person's own protection. Don't lose sight of the fact that we are talking about severe trauma happening to young children who are quite defenseless, trapped, and powerless to do much of anything about their situation. *The younger the child, the more frequent the abuse, the more brutal the abuse, and the closer the relationship of the abuser to the child, the more vulnerable and defenseless the child becomes, and the greater the intensity of the trauma.*

As time goes on, the memories remain in the unconscious, but the unconscious mind never really forgets. No doubt you have heard of people who, when facing an immediate crisis that may result in death, suddenly see their whole life played before them like a movie in fast-forward. The unconscious mind is at that moment playing back memories of the past that were forgotten. The unconscious mind has it all stored within, much like the hard disk of a computer. It's all there; we just need a way to access the information.

Then why can't the survivor just start looking within and dig out blocked memories to get past all these problems? It's not that simple. Tremendous mountains of shame, hurt, anger, and fear lurk in the shadows, threatening to come loose if the survivor starts to search out the memories. Furthermore, a certain part of the survivor is stuck in a child mode, a part that still reacts, thinks, and feels in the same vulnerable way of the child, and therefore feels helpless to work through the areas of trauma. Without professional therapeutic help, most survivors find it too difficult to work through the trauma alone.

What initially happens for most is that feelings of depression, anxiety, and sadness pervade. Because the survivor is now an adult and may actively be trying to understand what is going on within, the unconscious mind may allow limited bits of information and memory to leak through. Occasional flashes of images or pictures come to the mind that seem to indicate something terrible, but the memory seems remote, far away, and unreal. Recurring dreams and nightmares likewise give messages from the unconscious. Survivors of abuse often have nightmares of being chased, shot at, or about to be captured but somehow barely escaping. The survivor may be very sensitive to noises, certain smells, colors, or physical sensations and have no idea why. Here again memory fragments are leaking through the unconscious barrier, giving a few clues of much more to come.

Ron had appeared for ongoing therapy after a hospitalization for major depression. Things kept bothering him that he couldn't explain. Certain noises and sounds gave him a problem, sometimes getting him very upset. The noise could be a very simple thing—the crinkle of the bag as his wife ate potato chips could suddenly set him off. Even as we talked, he heard some noises outside the office door. Ron reacted suddenly: His body shook violently; his arms flew up close to his head, flailing away as if protecting himself from a severe attack. This reaction lasted for a minute or two and then faded away. I sat quietly. There was nothing dangerous happening. At first, Ron had no real explanation of what was going on. He was puzzled. He didn't understand this phenomenon at all.

As we continued to dig into his background, flashbacks of events from the past intruded into conscious memory. He gradually put together a picture of a very cruel mother who, the moment she came through the door, would find something wrong and attack and beat him unmercifully while he was still a young boy. He was terrified of her, and, therefore, just the sound of the key in the door would bring terror. The recurring scene of her entering the house and attacking him had made him very sensitive to sound, even hypervigilant. Although the actual memory of repeated trauma had long been buried, the hypervigilance and reaction to sound had remained as clues to a very unhappy childhood.

As we probed more deeply, the mental pictures expanded, indicating a dark figure with long scraggly hair, walking, tapping a stick. Ron's reaction was one of terror. He again shook with fear and trembling. The description did not fit his mother, but was more like his grandmother with whom they had lived for a while. This was puzzling. His memories of grandmother were positive, thus to be terrified of her did not fit his conscious memory.

In a later session, Ron brought up some dreams of a sexual nature with no idea where they came from. He had for years been turned off sexually until his hospital experience had helped him shed some of his inhibitions. Using some relaxation techniques, we were able again to dig into some bits of blocked memory. This time he again saw the same figure with the tapping noise made by a stick or swordlike object. Suddenly Ron went into violent shaking again, this time greatly upset. With difficulty he explained that this memory fragment involved something sexual. He was very embarrassed and felt a great deal of humiliation and shame. Although the memory pieces seemed remote and unreal, evidence mounted to indicate he had indeed been repeatedly beaten by his mother. Now new evidence pointed toward some sort of sexual abuse that involved his grandmother. It all seemed overwhelming, strange, and hard to accept.

What is really happening here? This is an example of *dissociation,* an act of defending oneself against the pain so that its memory is completely blocked, leaving only a blank spot where a trauma once was, with no hint of anything having happened.[2] Though the evidence mounts, the flashbacks increase, and the memory pieces of the abuse itself gradually come together, the survivor has difficulty believing the traumatic events were real.

Memory fragments include feelings such as intense shame and humiliation, tremendous fear, or pain that do not fit the situation at the moment. There may be sudden severe reactions that do not fit the present setting, indicating a body memory from an abusive past. Smells, sounds, color associations, and physical sensations all remain in permanent memory even though the events they are associated with have been long blocked off. Other examples could be a severe tightness of the throat, physical pain in private areas when nothing is happening, a severe reaction to the smell of a room or a person's aftershave, any of which could trigger terror and panic. One of my patients thanked me for never wearing a red shirt, although I had some in my closet, as her father almost always wore red when he abused her.

Because of severe trauma in the life of a young child, the mind builds an amnesiac barrier around the deep and overwhelming wounds so that there is no conscious memory of the events, thus enabling the child to survive psychologically. Only many years later do bits and pieces of memory begin to leak through, but none of these make much sense to the survivor until he or she is helped to put together the difficult puzzle of his or her life.

Other Related Illnesses

In addition to all the various manifestations of childhood sexual abuse described up to this point, we should consider some other types of disorders that may very well have their roots in childhood sexual abuse.

Mental Illness

Not everyone who has experienced severe abuse in their early years will necessarily dissociate those memories. Because of their own personality predisposition and biochemical makeup, some will suffer a break with reality and will retreat into one of the various forms of psychotic illness. Such a person may experience hallucinations, seeing things that are not real or hearing voices outside of his or her head. Or the person may experience thoughts that everyone is against him or her, that he or she is a person marked for punishment from others or from God. The problem at this point has become a biochemical imbalance in the brain and requires medicine as the primary treatment, along with supportive therapy. This type of person is unable to delve deeply into his or her abuse, the memories, the pain, and anguish within, as it could result in a total collapse. A much slower approach is called for, with a great deal of supportive help as a vital part of the healing process. Generally the assistance of a psychiatrist is required, at least for the medical part of the therapy.

Eating Disorders

Usually a problem of the young, the individual views self as ugly, fat, and unacceptable. Therefore, the individual may literally starve himself or herself in order to bring his or her weight down to an "acceptable" level, usually way below what is healthy and safe. This problem is called *anorexia*. Another related problem is that of *bulimia*, in which the person uses food as a tranquilizer to satisfy the inner hunger for love and caring. The resulting problem of weight gain is controlled by purging or vomiting the excess food. Either of these problems can be precipitated by childhood sexual abuse. The compulsive eating problem becomes a way of dealing with the emotional conflict.

Borderline Personality

Persons with borderline personality problems are individuals who move from one crisis to another. Their lives are in a great deal of turmoil. Sometimes the crisis is that of personal identity. Other times the person is subject to compulsions, driven toward certain behaviors that can be personally destructive. Their symptoms may shift from one type of problem to another. They impulsively act out what they feel and thus get themselves into all kinds of scrapes they regret, but they seem to have little power to avoid their problem behavior in the future. Their feelings are quite repressed, and they have little understanding of the real root of their problems. They may, therefore, resist the real focus of therapy by being fixated on a lot of side issues, rapidly changing from one viewpoint to another.

Gay or Lesbian Lifestyles

Homosexuality is a rather complex issue in which there are no easy answers. Identity issues are common to both homosexuality and survivors of sexual abuse where the abuse comes from a person of the same sex. A young boy sexually abused by an older male will indeed have masculine identity problems, but it should be clearly understood that this does not in itself constitute homosexuality, nor is the abuse a homosexual relationship. The child being abused is not choosing as a consenting adult to express his love toward the older male in a sexual way, nor does the abuser particularly think of the boy in homosexual terms, that of loving another male. The dynamics are that of *power over a child victim*. There are some homosexuals who have experienced childhood sexual abuse, to be sure, and their identity confusion has its origins in that abuse.

Addictions

Many survivors of childhood sexual abuse turn to alcohol, drugs, or some other addiction to help them escape the awful memories that won't go away. The alcohol or drugs act as an anesthesia to take away the pain and bury the memories. Since the pain returns as the effects of the substance wear off, the survivor must repeatedly drink or take drugs in order to escape the turmoil. As time goes on, the substance abuse becomes addicting, and the survivor then has to deal with an addictive problem as well as his or her own abuse. Self-control becomes lost. Other forms of addiction, such as gambling, eating, and even sexual addiction, may well be part of the same root problem.

It is important to note that none of the illnesses just listed can be assumed to have their origins in childhood sexual abuse. There are many other possible causes, and each problem must be sorted out as to its real roots and worked through accordingly.

Summary

How would you as the reader possibly know if you have been sexually abused in your early years? Certainly many survivors of sexual abuse have very clear memories of someone molesting them and have gone through all the feelings and struggles described in earlier chapters. Their experience was very vivid, and in fact, very hard to forget. Such is usually the case when the victimization has come in later childhood or early adolescence. The memories also tend to be somewhat more clear if the abuser was more removed from the direct family line, such as a neighbor, a respected friend of the family, baby-sitter, etc. The closer the family member, the more extensive the abuse, the more brutal the abuse, and the younger the child, the more likely that the trauma of the abuse is buried further below the level of consciousness. Any of these factors alone would make a difference in the survivor's ability to recall traumatic events, and the combination of all of these factors would have an even more profound effect in blocking the events from conscious memory.

See appendix A for some pertinent questions to help you determine whether abuse may have happened in your own life. But before you come to any conclusions, remember:

1. You cannot conclude childhood sexual abuse because your answers to two or three questions are positive.
2. Positive answers to most of the questions indicate only a probability, not an established fact. Further exploration is in order.
3. Don't panic, and don't jump to conclusions as to who may have molested you. Don't rush out with all kinds of accusations and confrontations until you really know for sure what happened, how often, when it happened, who the perpetrator really was, and what you can do about it in a sensible way. Get help from someone who is professionally trained and who does a lot of work in this area.

8

Dissociative Identity Disorder

The LORD is close to the brokenhearted
and saves those who are crushed in spirit.

I waited patiently for the LORD;
*   he turned to me and heard my cry.*
He lifted me out of the slimy pit,
*   out of the mud and mire;*
he set my feet on a rock
*   and gave me a firm place to stand.*
He put a new song in my mouth,
*   a hymn of praise to our God.*
Many will see and fear
*   and put their trust in the LORD.*

Psalms 34:18; 40:1–3

Betty complained of frequent headaches related to her inner turmoil and confusion. She talked about losses of time she couldn't account for. She might run into someone who said they had met in the mall and chatted for a while a few days earlier, yet she would have no recollection at all of seeing this person and not have a clue what they talked about. Betty had learned to cover up a lot but had an underlying fear that someone would discover her problem. Sometimes her husband would be upset with her, complaining that she was acting like a five-year-old, and there was a part of her like that. Betty feared that she might act that way in public and people would think she was really off. Sometimes she would find something she had written but have no recollection of it, even though it was obviously recent and in her own handwriting. Sometimes she would cut herself because at the time it seemed right and because somehow it relieved the extreme pressure inside of her. Sometimes she heard a multitude of voices inside of her head, like people arguing with each other. Betty did not seem to know what was going on.

After being in therapy for more than a year, one snowy night Betty came to my office. She brought a list of names of people. Most of them were children of different ages; some were adults. Each one of these persons had a specific function; all were a part of her, yet each was distinct from the others. Betty had Dissociative Identity Disorder, and she was scared that someone would find out and think she was crazy.

Perhaps the most bizarre and complex reaction to repeated childhood sexual abuse is that of the Dissociative Identity Disorder (DID), formerly known as Multiple Personality Disorder. The diagnosis of DID until recently was considered very rare. Because it was supposed that few therapists would ever be likely to see such a case in their lifetime, little emphasis was given to DID in training programs. Indeed, many seasoned therapists doubt that such a disorder even exists. However, therapists who are well tuned to the needs of survivors of sexual abuse are finding DID patients popping up with frightening frequency. Usually the patient does not reveal much of anything that would indicate such a diagnosis in the earlier stages of therapy. Only after enough strength has been gained and sufficient trust has developed in the process of therapy do they reveal clues that point in that direction.

Two separate studies about the early lives of people with Dissociative Identity Disorder came up with the same percentages: 97 percent of people with DID have been subjected to serious child abuse as youngsters. Another study found that 88 percent of DID patients had been abused sexually, with 83 percent having been abused as young children. Dissociation is used as a defense mechanism only when the pain has been extreme and when severe abuse has occurred usually in the preschool years. In order for dissociation to become a preferred coping style, which is the case in DID, the pain has to start in very early years, and dissociation has to be used often enough to become a habit.[1]

A general definition of Dissociative Identity Disorder, which is accepted by mental health professionals and used in all research and clinical settings, comes from *The Diagnostic and Statistical Manual of Mental Disorders* (DSM IV):

> Dissociative Identity Disorder (formerly Multiple Personality Disorder) is characterized by the presence of two or more distinct identities or personality states that recurrently take control of the individual's behavior accompanied by an inability to recall important personal information that is too extensive to be explained by ordinary forgetfulness.[2]

How could this state of affairs come to be? How can one person have several distinct personalities, any one of which may appear and dominate the whole person at any one time and cause the person to behave in a manner characteristic of that particular personality?

When a very young child is sexually abused, the terror can be so overwhelming that he or she splits off to another personality who does not experience the abuse. When the pain becomes too unbearable, another personality, or *alter* as they are often called, may split off to handle the pain so that the original child can cope with the abuse without feeling the pain. Another alter may carry the sadness, another the anger, another may feel hopeless and depressed, another is full of hatred, all so the child can be unaware of those overwhelming feelings and thus cope with life. Other alters may be formed later who know nothing of the abuse but help the individual cope with day-to-day life on an adult level. Another alter may assist the individual when help is needed; another may protect some of the younger alters from the outside world. Other alters may help the survivor deal with the adult world and its day-to-day demands. Each alter is unique in its personality and role in the system.

Generally, most Dissociative Identity Disorder individuals have a well-organized system of alters who enable the survivor to cope with life. Each alter serves an important function in the whole system and helps keep the system in balance. Each DID individual is unique, but generally they share some of the following:

> *The host personality.* This alter has executive control of the body the greatest percentage of the time. This one is trying to deal with the demands of everyday life, although often feeling overwhelmed and powerless, at the mercy of forces beyond his or her control or comprehension. This one is basically good, self-punishing, depressed, anxious, and has a variety of bodily symptoms, particularly headaches. Usually this personality has no knowledge of the past and strongly denies the existence of other alter personalities.
>
> *Child personalities.* Usually there are a number of child and infant personalities in DID individuals. The children are usually frozen in time, locked into a given age until late in their therapy. The age of each is tied to the time specific traumatic events took place. Once they have been relieved of their psychological burden, they may grow up. Each one holds pieces of memories and feelings produced by their traumatic experiences.
>
> *Persecutor personalities.* Many DID individuals have alters who sabotage their progress or may inflict serious injury upon the body in attempts to kill or injure one or more alters. These bring the greatest danger to the individual and may be responsible for mutilation or suicide. They believe they can kill another alter without endangering themselves.

Suicidal personalities. These may have no awareness of others but are driven to kill themselves as a single-minded task. They are so overwhelmed by a sense of hopelessness that they see death as the only way to escape their terrible suffering. The whole system of personalities can often be enlisted to keep the self-destructive impulses in check.

Protector and helper personalities. Most DID individuals have an array of helper personalities who serve as a counterbalance to the persecutor and suicidal alters. The protectors usually gain more influence and control as the individual becomes stronger. Some of them may be quite strong and powerful, able to overcome an outside person twice their size who is perceived to be threatening. Some of them may be male alters in a female individual.

The internal self-helper. This alter generally provides information and insights into the inner workings of the system and can be a very helpful guide in providing timely suggestions about problems and issues in therapy. This alter may also take over in times of internal crisis to avert a self-destructive act of another alter.

The memory trace personality. This passive alter has a more or less complete memory of the individual's life history but takes no active role.

The original personality. This identity develops just after birth and generates the first new personality in order to help the person survive a severe stress. This alter may be somewhat incapacitated at a very early age by not being able to cope with the trauma. This one may not emerge until late in the therapy after a lot of the trauma has been processed.[3]

Of course there are other alters. It is fairly common for an individual to have ten actively functioning alters. Other

DID individuals may have fifty or more. Some will have fewer than ten, all depending on the extent of the abuse, the age at onset, the brutality experienced, and the ability of the individual to dissociate and split off when faced with trauma. A whole complicated system thus develops to make it possible for a very damaged child to be able to survive in an adult world with all its demands and pressures. As time goes on, life gets more complicated, and the demands on the system become greater. Anxiety and depression increase, and the individual may seek out therapeutic help because the pressure becomes too great.

Unfortunately, the real problem of DID is frequently not recognized, and the individual is misdiagnosed even by seasoned therapists. The presence of voices within the person (one alter communicating with another) may be mistaken for a psychotic reaction, and the person is inappropriately hospitalized for mental illness. The use of antipsychotic drugs tends to bury the problem, but the individual basically does not get better. Another common scenario is that the individual is not taken seriously, is told that he or she is making this all up because such terrible things could never have happened. This kind of judgment only feeds into the survivor's already existing doubts; the trauma becomes even more deeply buried and the possibility of self-destruction even more real.

I wish you could see firsthand the horrendous suffering and agony these brave survivors experience as they recapture the memories and trauma of their abuse. It would be very real to you as well. The horrible experiences they relive are not things most people would even think about, much less make up. The reason the DID person has lingering doubts is because the dissociative process makes the memory seem so removed and distant as to seem unreal. Unless DID is correctly diagnosed and properly treated, the survivor does not get well.

Jill came to my office exhibiting symptoms of severe depression and anxiety. She had been to other therapists and had made no progress at all. The depression and anxiety persisted, and life had become increasingly difficult. Our attempts to dig into contributing problems kept coming to frustrating dead ends. She described a giant steel door that would slam down each time we would attempt to dig into the past.

However, as we worked on dreams (the language of the unconscious) and journaling (writing her thoughts and feelings), new clues began to point us in the right direction. Jill brought six pages of material each week. A lot of inner trauma seemed to be trying to come out. Interestingly enough, the style of the writing would change as the thoughts shifted. Some would be in ordinary cursive style, others in a child's printing, some in an intense scribbly style. When I asked about different parts of the written material, Jill had no conscious memory of the event described or even of having written it. The emerging memories that began to seep through pointed to two things: early childhood sexual abuse and Dissociative Identity Disorder. After her condition was properly diagnosed and the appropriate treatment approach had begun, Jill started to make slow but steady progress.

Because of the fact that individuals with Dissociative Identity Disorder readily switch from one personality to another, strange things happen that are hard to explain. The individual may get up in the morning and find pages of written manuscript in his or her own writing describing some event in his or her life but have no memory of having written it or of the event itself. Or a DID survivor may get to the end of the day with no recollection whatsoever of anything he or she did. A survivor may be very troubled at one point and go to see a therapist but have switched personalities by the time he or she gets there and have no recollection of what he or she was troubled about. A DID patient may have incredible fears that someone will discover the problem and proclaim him or her crazy, or that a child alter will come out at some inappropriate time and will do something very embarrassing. This individual may fear that an angry alter will come out and will hurt his or her own children, which sometimes does happen.

Betty recounted her recent experience with a toothache. The tooth was really bothering her, but since she couldn't get an immediate appointment with the dentist, she handled it by switching to another personality who didn't feel any pain. Her only problem was that once she finally did get to the dentist, she no longer felt the pain. Nor could she recall which tooth was giving a problem. The dentist couldn't help her.

At another time, Betty called from her job in desperation. She had a once-a-month accounting procedure to do, but the intelligent adult personality who usually handled her day-to-day working skills wasn't out or available. Betty couldn't remember how to do the procedure. Panic set in. I helped her to calm down and become more patient with her problem. Usually DID people have a helper alter who either comes to the rescue or sends someone out who can do the job. Sure enough, the next day the intelligent host alter returned and did the task with ease and in plenty of time.

Jill was trying hard to meet the challenges of being a parent to a very strong-willed daughter who pushed every limit, expressed hatred for her mother, refused to do what she was told, and became generally very hard to manage. Jill would become very frustrated and upset, seeing herself as a failure as a mother because she had little control over this child.

Strong-willed kids need a lot of consistency and firmness from the parent to help with their own impulsiveness and lack of self-control. However, because the events of the day were often a total blank to Jill, she could not recall whether the daughter had been obedient or rebellious. Because the daughter did not experience the needed firmness from Jill, she further manipulated the scene to suit her own interests.

One of the main tasks of therapy for a DID individual is to make available to the entire system of personalities the knowledge and secrets held by specific alter personalities. As bits of memories and flashbacks are gradually put together, the main events of the survivor's abuse take shape and the related feelings are released. Then the need for separate personalities gradually erodes, and the movement toward resolution begins.[4] Reintegration or restoration of the wholeness of the person then becomes possible.

As we try to put ourselves in the shoes of a DID person, we can only begin to see some of their nightmare just to get through each day, not to mention the ordeal of digging up traumatic memories of the past in order to get well. Theirs is indeed a perilous journey, and some of them would rather live with DID than work through the pain required to get well. They need all the support and encouragement that we can give them.

Satanic Ritual Abuse

No discussion of childhood sexual abuse and Dissociative Identity Disorder would be complete without some words about Satanic Ritual Abuse (SRA). If there are few experts dealing with DID, there are even fewer with SRA. Authoritative material on the subject is very sketchy, and there is still considerable debate about the reality of SRA. Overwhelming evidence from clinical sources, however, point toward terrible things happening involving not only brutal child sexual abuse, but ritual sacrifices of animals and humans as well. If you think that repeated forcible rape of a small child by a family member is unthinkable, SRA is far worse, being the most hideous of all child abuse. The basic objective in SRA is to so terrorize and methodically torture children in a premeditated and systematic way with well-thought-out rituals that the child is caused to dissociate and thus develop multiple personalities in order to survive. Why do they want the child to dissociate? So that the child will have no conscious memory of the extensive abuse and atrocities that follow. Thus a child can be made to continue in their rituals for years and have no conscious awareness of what is happening. Only many years later do flashbacks and fragments of memory leak through to conscious awareness.

In order to produce Dissociative Identity Disorder in children, the ritual abusers put the child through experiences in which he or she believes death is imminent. The child may first be wounded with some type of body mutilation, then buried alive in a coffin or box and left for a few days, expecting to die. Or the child may be placed in a plastic bag and held underwater until death seems imminent. Being brought out alive may be part of "being born into the cult," or being "born unto Satan." The terror of these experiences is too much for a young child to handle psychologically, and the mind creates other personalities to help the child survive. Once DID is in place, the cult has prepared the child to cope with the terrors and atrocities that follow as part of their rituals. Because the child splits off to other personalities to survive, and a complete amnesiac blockage exists, the child has no conscious memory of what really took place. The identity of the perpetrators is thus safeguarded from prosecution.[5]

Once in therapy, the memories and flashbacks may come in layers. The earlier memories may be of incest, then may come memories of robes and candles, then there may be memories of either or both parents present and participating in the abuse of the child. Another layer of memories may be that of seeing adults, children, and babies hurt and even killed. Another layer brings back memories of being forced to participate in the sacrifices, the most painful being that of having to sacrifice one's own baby, born because of repeated rape.

Flashbacks for Satanic Ritual Abuse victims may seem even more strange than those of ordinary Dissociative Identity Disorder survivors. Such things as panic associated with water, mice, tunnels, knives, colors of red or black, candles, or sensations around the throat, back of the neck, shoulders, or private areas all may be associated with some sort of ritualistic abuse. For example, a memory fragment of an SRA victim may bring the sensation of a very stiff and cold arm, accompanied with a lot of fear. A child alter may later explain that the child had been forced to kill an animal in a ritual murder and was very scared about what was happening. Further exploration may indicate that the child was forced to help kill another child victim.

As memories surface, the survivor feels he or she is in total turmoil, as though a war of good and evil were going on. There are alters within who believe they have given themselves to Satan and feel there is no hope for them. Indeed, SRA victims have been indoctrinated to believe this to be the case. The child is repeatedly told while in a suggestible state that he or she is evil. This may be done by undermining the victim's trust of his or her senses through the use of drugs, electric shock, hypnosis, torture, rape, humiliation, illusion, long periods of isolation (such as being locked in a box or closet), deprivation of food, sleep, or water, partial drowning, or being hanged by the hands or feet.[6] The use of such techniques puts the child into an even more suggestible state and more susceptible to destructive and aggressive impulses arising from within.[7]

One of the most important components is the establishment of guilt in the victim. The adults in the group force the child to commit atrocities and then point out how evil the young child must have been to have done these things. The child may be forced to hold a knife and stab something living. The adult may then stand back and say, "Look at what you just did." The child may be forced to perform sex acts with animals, other children, or adults or to participate in pornography as a way to convince the child that he or she is evil. The child may be forced to participate in a ritual where another child is injured or killed. The child may be told that because he or she resisted a cult request, someone else close to the child will be punished. Thus, when the child resists what he or she feels is immoral, the child is made to feel the other person is suffering because of the child's actions. The only safe way, then, is to comply with whatever the cult requests.[8]

Some survivors report having been manually stimulated sexually by their abusers while being forced to watch or participate in atrocities. Then they were accused of being evil because they were aroused while another was being hurt. The child frequently blames himself or herself for what occurs, thus resulting in a tormented individual who views self as evil, culpable, and dangerously out of control.[9]

In the Satanic Ritual Abuse thought reform process, there is a consistent use of "the breaking point" deliberately induced by torture. Cult members may beat the victims, fracture their limbs, and/or rape them repeatedly until the break occurs. The most common form of the break is through dissociation and DID. Most SRA victims report fears of annihilation that have been deliberately induced by their abusers.[10]

What is the reason for all of this madness? Why would people stoop to such brutality? The underlying reason seems rooted in the *greed for power*, similar to the motivating force behind child abuse. The sense of power is found in preying on others. Many Satanists believe that a relationship exists between incest, magic, idolatry, sacrifice, and the consumption of blood. They therefore assume that forbidden incestuous relationships, the consumption of blood, and human sacrifice all provide the power to do magic. In occult theory, a living creature is a storehouse of energy, and when the victim is killed, most of the energy is suddenly liberated and out of proportion to the size or strength of the victim. The task of the magician is to unleash the power through the sacrifice so that all who stand within the circle will benefit.[11] The newfound power allegedly enables the coven member to accomplish all kinds of things in life without fear of being found out.

Most Satanic Ritual Abuse victims have been brainwashed to believe they or someone close to them will die or their house will be burned if they don't do what they are told. Since they have seen others killed, SRA victims have every reason to believe the threats. They are often suicidal because they believe they might as well kill themselves if they disobey the dire warning, rather than wait for the cult to kill them. Most are programmed to report to someone in the cultic coven by a preprogrammed signal on the telephone or by meeting someone from the group who takes the victim to the coven leader. The victim is then reduced to a compliant child to report what he or she has done or revealed. Threats of death may follow, or the victim may kill himself or herself at their command. Thus the threat of death or suicide becomes a serious matter with survivors of Satanic Ritual Abuse even more so than with Dissociative Identity Disorder.

As strange as it may seem, the survivor of SRA, with all of the atrocities and horror that he or she has experienced, may go into the teen and early adult years with no recollection whatsoever of the terrible things that happened. The survivor may appear to be rather normal, with no indications that anything is really wrong. Eventually small fragments of memory or flashbacks of weird or frightening scenes enter the conscious mind. Strange physical reactions to seemingly harmless events, smells, or colors take place with no logical explanation. Huge gaps of memory appear; strange switches in outward personality may be manifested. The survivor's fear of losing control intensifies, anxiety lev-

els become high, depression takes over. Hopefully the survivor seeks professional help at this point.

Truth versus Imagination

At the time of this writing, a major debate rages as to
whether repressed memories of early childhood sexual
abuse are real and accurate or are made up by the victim or
even invented by the therapist through the power of suggestion. A very interesting and enlightening series of articles
was published in the September/October 1993 issue of *The
Family Therapy Networker*[12] on the various aspects of this
debate. On one side are the members of the False Memory
Society Foundation, parents who say they have been falsely
accused of molesting their children, who maintain that the
memories their offspring claim to be fact are indeed figments
of their imagination or major embellishments of family un-
rest. Parents in this group insist that such acts never happened, nor can they understand how such terrible accusations have come from once happy and caring children. Most
of the blame is aimed at therapists who are allegedly putting
ideas into the minds of their clients. They cite the testimony
of some who have accused their parents but who have now
recanted, blaming their therapists for leading them on in the
belief that they were indeed abused and pressuring them to
produce memories of abuse. As a result families have been
splintered and torn apart, and reputations and careers ruined because of the serious accusations hurled at them.[13]

Likewise, researchers in memory are casting doubt on
the accuracy of memory. Elizabeth Loftus, an eminent authority on cognitive process and eyewitness memory, cites
extensive research—her own and that of others—that demonstrates how subject memory is to inaccuracy, fabrication,
confusion, and alteration. She argues that repressed memories of childhood sexual abuse—the sole source of criminal
and civil charges against many parents—may well be en-

tirely false, the product of the therapist's suggestion and the client's imagination. "At this point, nobody can distinguish between false and real memories without external corroboration," says Loftus. "Accepting all repressed memories as literally true, no matter how dubious . . . is bound to lead to an increased likelihood that society in general will disbelieve the genuine cases of childhood sexual abuse that truly deserve our sustained attention."[14]

Many therapists who work with sexual abuse and Dissociative Identity Disorder clients express an equal suspicion of the False Memory Society and its mysterious sources of funding as a media-directed organization that manipulates its member families and is dedicated to putting out disinformation. Therapists point out that anguish is not any more convincing from a parent than from an abused child. Denial can come from either side, for there is plenty of evidence to show there are survivors who deny having been abused even though there is ample medical evidence on record to prove the contrary.

As in any profession, there may be therapists who are unethical and may convince a client of memories that are not real. However, such therapists are a tiny minority.

Most therapists are not looking for all kinds of abuse under every rock, but the severity and complexity of the survivor's pathology and the tangible quality of his or her pain makes an extraordinary impression on even initially skeptical therapists. Nor do therapists enjoy listening to horrible tales of abuse. The unendurable agony of the clients that would be impossible to fake is the most powerful evidence for the truth of their experiences. Many of the clients would do anything to be able to deny or block their memories because they are absolutely shattering. For the therapist, the sense of their pain is sufficient; not every detail has to be believed or proven.[15]

Christine A. Courtois, author of *Healing the Incest Wound*, suggests that the controversy over "false memories" is a part of a backlash against the long-delayed social acknowledgment of widespread sex abuse, and the "whole-sale degradation of psychotherapy by some delayed memory critics" represents "displaced rage" at therapists for bringing the issue to public attention. She is also skeptical about the relevance of cognitive memory research to clinical practice with abuse survivors. "There is data to suggest that traumatic memory is psychologically encoded differently than normal memory," she says. "I think we have to be very careful about drawing conclusions about trauma memory from lab studies of ordinary memory, conducted on nontraumatized volunteers, usually college students who might be doing it for class credit, or getting paid. We cannot apply these experiences wholesale to the issue of traumatic memory."[16]

Therapists are in a dilemma. A therapist can be sued for not asking the right questions and thus not treating the real problem. The therapist can also be sued for asking too many questions, and thus "leading" the client. This battle will rage on for a long time to come. There are extremes on either side. Meanwhile there are hundreds of thousands of victims who desperately want and need our help. They do not need further disbelief, which only once again blames the victim and sets all of us back many years to when no one would talk of such matters. Nor do we need to assume that every victim remembers every last detail with perfect accuracy. The task of the therapist is to assist the survivor seeking help to work through the deep suffering and anguish within and to point the way to health and happiness. The debates are not the main issue. *The victims' stories must be heard, and they must be helped.*

Summary

Some people who were subjected to severe abuse at a very early age may have serious difficulty recalling any of those events until bits and pieces seep through in later adult life. What little information comes through may be confused, grossly incomplete, and very disturbing. They may suffer intense pain with little idea of where it is coming from. Such is the case with Dissociative Identity Disorder, Satanic Ritual Abuse, and other dissociative disorders where there is a total amnesia block from extensive abuse at a young age. These survivors are desperately looking for help, and there are few who understand their real problem. Debates about the credibility of the retrieved memories do not help to relieve the survivors' suffering but only make that suffering more intense. They want you to try to understand, as confusing as their story may sound. Belief and acceptance is very important to them. They need you to be their friend.

Part 4
Finding Healing

9

The Confessional Process

The Spirit of the Sovereign LORD is on me,
because the LORD has anointed me
to preach good news to the poor.
He has sent me to bind up the brokenhearted,
to proclaim freedom for the captives
and release from darkness for the prisoners,
to proclaim the year of the LORD's favor
and the day of vengeance of our God,
to comfort all who mourn.

Isaiah 61:1–2

Years ago I worked as a car mechanic while in school. Most of the repair jobs were fairly straightforward. A few of them were strange, especially with new cars. Some from the factory had no oil; some had a double amount. I recall one that came in with a vague rubbing sound in the engine. No big deal, right? I listened carefully in different places as the engine idled. The sound was hard to isolate, but I finally decided that it was coming from inside the lower part of the engine. I removed the oil pan. Looking around inside, I found something very unusual. A large groove had been worn in the crankshaft. For some reason, the oil pump that delivers the motor oil throughout the engine was coming apart. One of the shafts in the oil pump had worked loose in its housing and had protruded enough to touch the crankshaft as it turned, thereby wearing the groove in the crankshaft with each revolution. The engine had to come out, be dismantled, and have the damaged parts replaced.

Needless to say the owner was a bit upset to see the engine from his brand-new car lying in many pieces on the floor.

There is no way the owner could nurse that new car along. Forgiving the person who made the faulty oil pump would not correct the problem. Nor could he just go on as if nothing had ever happened. Neither the shine of a new car nor a kindly spirit would be enough to make the car run properly. The entire engine would have been destroyed if he had ignored the problem. There was only one answer. *Get at the root problem no matter how painful, and fix it.*

Such is the task of confession: Admit there is a problem. Search for the problem until it is found. Face it squarely. Process, that is, work through what is found. Keep working at it until the damage is repaired and a lasting solution is reached.

Hope for Healing

Can I get better? Will I ever find a normal life? Would I know a normal life if I found it? Can I find genuine love, someone who respects me as a person and will not take advantage of me? Can I ever have a fulfilling marriage and a wholesome family? Can I even find someone I can trust? Can I ever be free from the guilt and shame that I feel? Can the pain really go away? Can I ever find a fulfilling life out there somewhere? Can things really go right for me? Will I ever laugh again? How long will it take?

These are questions in the mind of every survivor of sexual abuse. They desperately want a better life than what they have known most of their years, but they don't know where to find it or how to get started. Their deep emotional scars invade every part of their lives. They have gotten so used to just existing, they aren't sure that anything could be different for them.

The good news is that the ugly scars of abuse can heal. Genuine love and trust can be found. A life of fulfillment is within reach. Yes, there can be joy and happiness even for the sexually abused child grown into the now struggling adult.

What is the healing process, and what makes it seem so difficult at times? Why does the journey back sometimes seem worse than the abuse? There are no magical solutions. Healing is not sudden. Changes come slowly; the journey back is not easy. But hope for healing starts first with taking the time to find the real problem.

Get at the Roots

Weeds are every gardener's enemy. They sneak in at night while the gardener sleeps and threaten the fruits of his or her labor. In days gone by, I made valiant efforts to instill a sense of responsibility in my children through the grand task of pulling weeds in our garden. Since they would be the recipients of the firstfruits of our labor, how fitting that they should share in the process of producing a harvest. Reluctantly they complied with the boring task. When they had finally finished, behold, not a weed could be seen. None, that is, until a few days later when they all popped up again. What happened?

In their youthful enthusiasm, not to mention the desire to get me off their backs, they had removed all appearance of weeds. But they had overlooked something. These pesky little critters had something called roots. The main body of the weeds lay well below the surface of the ground. Unless the weeds were pulled out down to the roots, they would sprout up again in short order. A lot more careful work was needed to coax the roots from the soil and thus complete the job.

Healing of trauma in early developmental years involves getting at the roots of the problem. Skirting over the top with surface attention will not do the job. Digging out the roots can be a formidable task. As the survivor begins to face the traumas of the past, old feelings of fear, helplessness, anger, and pain come to the surface. Old forgotten memories come again into conscious awareness. The survivor now feels like a sailor in the storm, tossed about with waves crashing on every side and no land in sight.

"But why can't God just heal the past, remove the memories, and let me move on with my life?" the survivor may ask. God could do that. God could likewise dissolve a cancerous tumor deep within a person's body without surgery or treatment. In some miraculous way, sudden healing could take place. Occasionally such miracles do indeed happen, but such divine intervention does not come to most of us in that way.

Getting at the roots of the problem in childhood sexual abuse may not be easy. Some survivors have very clear memories of just what happened and are able to describe it all in sufficient detail if they have to. Not a pleasant task. But others are not so fortunate. Because their trauma was more extensive or happened at a much earlier age by someone close to the family, the memories are harder to find. Most of the trauma is deeply submerged, and since the conscious mind has blocked it all these years, it will be difficult to find the roots of the problem. But find it we must, for none of us can fix something we can't even see. Therefore, the first step in healing is that of *finding* the problem.

Aids for Finding the Problem

Ask God for Help

The psalmist David recognized the difficulty in getting at the problem. He prayed,

> Search me, O God, and know my heart;
>   test me and know my anxious thoughts.
> See if there is any offensive way in me,
>   and lead me in the way everlasting.
>   Psalm 139:23–24

David recognized he couldn't do this alone but needed help

from God. The thoughts didn't just come to him that easily; the conscious awareness was not all there.

Whether the "offensive way" David refers to is something he did wrong in deed or attitude, or whether the problem was inflicted by someone else, the principle is the same. We can pray for help to find the things we need to know, to discover the truth. Because most of my patients are Christians, I invite them to seek help from God to find the answers they need and for the ability to dig out the dark memories so that healing can take place.

Old Photos

Sometimes help can be found in recapturing old memories of what things were really like from old photos of the survivor and family at different ages. The survivor can look at pictures of himself or herself at different ages and see changes in his or her countenance.

As a survivor, I learned something in reviewing old photos of myself. Early pictures were of a happy young child who seemed normal and carefree. Pictures of myself from early adolescence onward took on a different light; early signs of insecurity became visible. As the age represented by the photos progressed, I saw in my facial expressions anger, tension, and extreme seriousness. The happiness was gone. I could now connect the changes in the photos with my abuse in adolescence.

Betty brought to me her school picture from about grade three. Although Betty did not see it at first, she seemed a very unhappy girl. Her facial expressions were clearly that of sadness and grief. Her expressions fit well with the torment of her home life at that age.

Drawings

For the more creative survivors, drawings and paintings of their feelings or just scenes that come to their mind can be very helpful in bringing out feelings and memories. Anyone who works with children knows that their drawings can readily represent significant events and feelings in their lives. Some may not be able to draw anything more than stick figures, but even these can give information from within. Sometimes drawing floor plans of the place where the abuse took place can bring back memories that need to surface.

> Jill shyly handed me a simple drawing. She was somewhat embarrassed and felt it was stupid. She had no idea what it meant or how it connected with anything. On paper was a simple sketch of a heart. But the heart was torn down the middle, pierced by a knife. Only later did she connect the drawing with the severe pain from deep within and the sense of her heart being broken and pierced from her father's abominable abuse. The picture told the story.

Talking about the Memories

Help can often be found by talking with other family members or relatives if they are supportive. Mental pictures or flashbacks of people or situations may seem very unreal or provide only bits of information. Another family member may be able to fill in details that affirm that the bits of memory are indeed real and accurate, just incomplete. However, such discussions must be handled with care, as there are many potential negative reactions from family that could make the whole process more difficult than it already is.

Having a close, confidential friend with whom the survivor can share his or her thoughts, feelings, and concerns is extremely valuable toward getting further down the road of recovery. The benefits are twofold. Just being able to talk openly and confidentially helps the survivor to release more and more of what needs to come out. Also, having such a friend wards off the loneliness and isolation to which most survivors tend to gravitate.

Support Groups

Increasingly available are support groups where other survivors gather to encourage and assist each other. The camaraderie of survivors sharing their own experiences together, helping each other through difficult periods, and forming a group identity with others struggling with the same problem can be very valuable. The experience that one survivor shares may trigger thoughts and feelings in another that were not previously accessible, and the group helps each other in processing those new discoveries. Therapy groups do all of this as well, but they are guided by a professional to specifically focus on the underlying issues of the abuse, releasing of powerful emotions, and specific step-by-step healing as appropriate for each survivor in the group.

Dreams

Keeping record of dreams can be very useful. Dreams give clues of what is happening beneath the surface of conscious awareness. When we sleep, our conscious mind is at rest, but our unconscious mind continues to chug away trying to help us resolve problems. Although some of the details of a dream may be related to something we experienced earlier in the day, the main theme of the dream may well reflect some underlying problems as yet unresolved. Dreams with recurring themes are even clearer messages of an underlying life problem.

Jill dreamed of finding an old doll in the trash in front of her house. The china doll head remained intact, but every other part of the doll was tattered, worn, and limp. The doll had obviously been through a great deal of use and abuse. As she thought about the dream, she realized the doll represented herself as a young child. Her severe abuse at an early age had taken its toll on her view of herself as a person. She now saw herself as worthless, her value as a piece of junk to be cast aside forever. She wept. The dream said it all.

Information

The survivor needs to read books, articles, and printed material from reputable authors on the subject of childhood sexual abuse. Conferences on the subject of abuse can be very useful. The survivor can obtain a great deal of valuable information through using these resources to develop a good understanding of the dynamics of abuse, its effects on its victims, how other survivors normally think and act, and ideas on overcoming the scars of abuse. Survivors are so isolated from others that they don't realize that most of what they think and feel is experienced by a host of others as well. To understand where the vast array of confusing feelings is coming from, to realize they have a clearly defined origin and cause, is in itself encouraging. It can help survivors begin to think a lot more positively about themselves when they can realize they are not as seriously defective as they once thought and recognize that many of their feelings about themselves are twisted as a direct result of the abuse. There is no substitute for truth as a valuable part of healing.

Journal Writing

Most survivors find real help in journal writing about feelings, thoughts, and memories that come to them. The survivor needs to get a notebook and write his or her private thoughts and feelings on a regular basis—daily if possible. The survivor needs to write about events he or she can recall, thoughts that may come, flashes of memory no matter how insignificant or even ridiculous they may seem. The survivor should pay particular attention to the feelings that go with the memories and write these also. Although the bits and pieces may at first seem like a big jumble, something like pieces of a jigsaw puzzle just out of the box, experience shows they do fit together in a clear, composite whole. Each piece is related to another, and eventually the whole picture becomes clear and plain. The confusion fades away.

> Jennifer presented symptoms of severe depression and inner confusion, but she had no idea what the trouble really was. As we prayed together and as she worked on journal writing of her thoughts, feelings, and dreams, we were gradually able to piece together the trauma of her past. She found memories that included a very emotionally abusive mother and a sexually abusive brother.
>
> The trauma of those years had severely damaged her as a child, but Jennifer had successfully buried all of it from conscious memory. However, as an adult the symptoms of depression and anxiety were so discomforting and paralyzing that she had to find help and healing. Each session was painful, but only as she got at the roots of the problem could real healing take place. After one and a half years of weekly therapy, sufficient healing had taken place for her to not only return with her family to their ministry overseas but to continue for years afterward.

Help from the Psalms

The process of journal writing is actually very similar to the writing of the Psalms. The psalmist pours out his inner thoughts and feelings in writing, and it becomes a part of his healing. Consider these examples:

Fear

> The cords of death entangled me;
>   the torrents of destruction overwhelmed me.
> The cords of the grave coiled around me;
>   the snares of death confronted me.
> In my distress I called to the LORD;
>   I cried to my God for help.

From his temple he heard my voice;
   my cry came before him, into his ears.

He reached down from on high and took hold of me;
   he drew me out of deep waters.
He rescued me from my powerful enemy,
   from my foes, who were too strong for me.
They confronted me in the day of my disaster,
   but the LORD was my support.
He brought me out into a spacious place;
   he rescued me because he delighted in me.
                                        Psalm 18:4–6, 16–19

David wrote of fear, because it was very much a part of his life as it is for each of us. As he wrote about his fears, overwhelming as they were, even to the point of death, he again found strength in his God. His fears diminished.

Helplessness

Hear my cry for mercy
   as I call to you for help,
as I lift up my hands
      toward your Most Holy Place.
Do not drag me away with the wicked,
   with those who do evil,
who speak cordially with their neighbors
   but harbor malice in their hearts.
Repay them for their deeds
   and for their evil work;
repay them for what their hands have done
   and bring back upon them what they deserve.

Praise be to the LORD,
   for he has heard my cry for mercy.
The LORD is my strength and my shield;
   my heart trusts in him, and I am helped.
                                        Psalm 28:2–4, 6–7

In this psalm, as in many others, the writer first presents his deepest feelings. As he pours it all out in writing, his perspective begins to change. He comes full circle to realize that God is his help. He is not alone. There is hope.

Guilt and Shame

The psalmist David experienced times of guilt and shame in his life, sometimes to the point of being overwhelmed with despair. He writes,

> Save me, O God,
>> for the waters have come up to my neck.
> I sink in the miry depths,
>> where there is no foothold.
> I have come into the deep waters;
>> the floods engulf me.
> I am worn out calling for help;
>> my throat is parched.
> My eyes fail,
>> looking for my God.
>
> You know my folly, O God;
>> my guilt is not hidden from you.
>
> But I pray to you, O LORD,
>> in the time of your favor;
> in your great love, O God,
>> answer me with your sure salvation.
> Rescue me from the mire,
>> do not let me sink;
> deliver me from those who hate me,
>> from the deep waters.
>
> Do not hide your face from your servant;
>> answer me quickly, for I am in trouble.
> Come near and rescue me;
>> redeem me because of my foes.
>
> Psalm 69:1–3, 5, 13–14, 17–18

As the psalmist continues to write, we see the mood
change from one who is loaded down with guilt to the point
of despair to one who is full of joy and thanksgiving. He
goes on to say,

> I will praise God's name in song
>   and glorify him with thanksgiving.
> This will please the LORD more than an ox,
>   more than a bull with its horns and hoofs.
> The poor will see and be glad—
>   you who seek God, may your hearts live!
> The LORD hears the needy
>   and does not despise his captive people.
>   Psalm 69:30–33

Anger

The psalm writer, this time Asaph, describes what so
many of us feel about injustices of the world and wickedness
around us. This may be especially pertinent to the survivor
of sexual abuse who has been severely violated.

> But as for me, my feet had almost slipped;
>   I had nearly lost my foothold.
> For I envied the arrogant
>   when I saw the prosperity of the wicked.
> They have no struggles;
>   their bodies are healthy and strong.
> They are free from the burdens common to man;
>   they are not plagued by human ills.
> Therefore pride is their necklace;
>   they clothe themselves with violence.
>
> They scoff, and speak with malice;
>   in their arrogance they threaten oppression.
> Their mouths lay claim to heaven
>   and their tongues take possession of the earth.
> Therefore their people turn to them
>   and drink up waters in abundance.

They say, "How can God know?
    Does the Most High have knowledge?"
This is what the wicked are like—
    always carefree, they increase in wealth.
                                Psalm 73:2–6, 8–12

From his own anger, the psalmist continues,

Surely in vain have I kept my heart pure;
    in vain have I washed my hands in innocence.
All day long I have been plagued;
    I have been punished every morning.

When I tried to understand all this,
    it was oppressive to me
till I entered the sanctuary of God;
    then I understood their final destiny.
Surely you place them on slippery ground;
    you cast them down to ruin.
How suddenly are they destroyed,
    completely swept away by terrors!

When my heart was grieved
    and my spirit embittered,
I was senseless and ignorant;
    I was a brute beast before you.
                        Psalm 73:13–14, 16–19, 21–22

His final conclusion,

Those who are far from you will perish;
    you destroy all who are unfaithful to you.
But as for me, it is good to be near God.
    I have made the Sovereign LORD my refuge;
I will tell of all your deeds.
                                Psalm 73:27–28

The psalmist writes of his anger at the injustice and mistreatment that has been his. He expresses that anger, even

beyond seemingly appropriate limits, and yet he is not judged. He gets it all out, and as he does, his perspective changes. He sees the plan of God for the destruction of the wicked, and his faith is renewed.

Writing what we feel can help each of us as well. We may get very upset at times and lose our perspective. We have the same anger at injustices toward us. Sometimes we feel rage beyond the limits of what seems appropriate. Writing what we feel helps us to focus our problem and regain our perspective on life.

As a survivor myself, I can remember times when I was weighed down with despair. I was never really sure where it came from and why the heaviness didn't go away. Just trying to get my mind on other things did not really do the job; the heaviness came back. Sometimes a pervasive anger bubbled within, and many things would irritate me that were not normally problems of any consequence. As I read the Psalms of David, they spoke to my heart. I could see how the burden upon the psalmist's heart would change as he poured out his innermost feelings. Maybe there was a principle here that could be helpful. I began to keep a private journal. I would go to a quiet place where I could meditate and think. I wrote what came from inside my heart.

As I wrote, no matter how bad it sounded, I noted that my spirits lifted. Despair turned to singing, anger turned to peace, discouragement turned to optimism, fear and helplessness turned to courage, so that I could take hold of situations and carry out appropriate action. It seemed like a gift from God. Moreover, I was able to identify more clearly the focus of my feelings. Many of them originated from my abuse years ago but were being stirred up by situations from the present. As I was able to sort out the roots of the problem, I was able to discern which feelings came from which sources and just what I needed to do about it. I felt a lot more in charge of my everyday life, for now I could react more appropriately to things that came my way.

Dissociation

For those with dissociative disorders, including Dissociative Identity Disorder and Satanic Ritual Abuse, the journal writing methods described above are useful but not entirely adequate. The amnesiac barrier is too strong to get at a lot of the vital information and feelings. The memories are too well guarded and protected because of the severity of the trauma at a very early age. At first there will be no memory at all, only huge gaps in what was once a childhood. Therefore, some survivors may be able to get only bits and pieces of memory, a few flashbacks, and some emotional reactions they cannot understand, but not nearly enough to put anything together in any meaningful way. While others will talk of events in their own childhood, survivors with a dissociative disorder can only listen and wonder. "Why don't I remember that period of my life? Is there something really wrong with my mind?" The DID/SRA survivor will need a lot of help getting at the truth of past trauma. The memories can be found, but it takes more to get them out. The journey will be long and difficult, but the truth will set us free.

A therapist who has been trained to work with dissociative disorders can be very helpful. The survivor has to be helped to relax and concentrate very deeply, to be able to shut out all outside distractions, and to find the door to the inner parts of the mind. Long-forgotten scenes will begin to appear as the survivor is able to visualize scenes of many years ago. Many of these memories will be uncomfortable and unsettling, but each scene will fit with the others like pieces in a puzzle. The reliving of these lost memories will seem very real while the survivor is experiencing the memory, but they will fade into the distance when the person returns to conscious awareness of the present.

Jill was able to relax as she visualized a large field of flowers, blue skies, and fluffy clouds overhead. As Jill thought on the scene, it became as though she were actually there. A short distance away was a bench where a person was sitting. Jesus was there, watching. The scene was peaceful and safe.

Suddenly, out of the field came a little girl, hardly much taller than the flowers. She seemed so small. Her face looked like a doll's, very similar to the china doll Jill had dreamed about before—the one in the trash. The little girl moved toward her. Her eyes were wide; her face was expressionless; she did not speak. The girl looked like she was in shock from some kind of trauma. Jill put her arm around the little girl, who relaxed some, and they sat together until it was time to leave.

Jill did not understand all that was happening here, but she had actually gone deep into her memory, had changed to an earlier age, and had met a very little girl who was an even younger version of herself. Each person represented a different age; each had different but incomplete memories of terrible things that happened; neither was much aware of the other or believed they even were a part of each other. Jill had Dissociative Identity Disorder.

As Jill was helped to visit the inner recesses of her mind, she was able to find other personalities, or alters, who were part of her, each of whom had part of the memory and truth, some with memories of events, some with memories of feelings. As the different alters were helped to work through their own feelings, misconceptions, and memories, the wide gaps between the different personalities narrowed, and they were able to communicate with each other. The whole system began working together more as a unit, and Jill became stronger as a person. Healing was taking place.

The healing process for a Satanic Ritual Abuse victim is similar in most ways to that for Dissociative Identity Disor-

der, because most of them are DID also. The uncovering of
SRA memories becomes extremely difficult because they are
so horrible. The same methods are used as with the DID
survivor, but some things are different. There is still plenty
of debate as to the reality of the satanic component in these
persons' lives. Some will argue that a persecutor alter can be
mistaken for a demon, but a growing number of therapists
are taking the demonic aspects of SRA survivors rather seriously. Many are adding the methods of spiritual warfare
to deal with demonic components of the SRA survivor. The
personal safety of the survivor is of primary concern because many SRA victims have been programmed to expect
death or to kill themselves if they tell about their experiences. As a Christian therapist helping a survivor of SRA, I
should be certain of the following.

- the strength of my own spiritual life
- good prayer backing from other believers
- readiness to call on the power of God to cast out a
  demon when and if one or more could be identified

Helping SRA victims is not for the fainthearted, nor is it
something to be attempted entirely on your own. Even an
experienced therapist will need support both through
prayer and backup in order to do this work.

Healing through Truth

Isn't there an easier way? Does a person who has been
through childhood sexual abuse have to go back through
those awful memories in order to be healed?

Although not identical, there is a close parallel to be
found in the biblical teaching about confession. The most
direct instruction is found in two New Testament passages:

> If we confess our sins, he is faithful and just and will forgive
> us our sins and purify us from all unrighteousness.
>   1 John 1:9

> Therefore confess your sins to each other and pray for each other so that you may be healed.
>
> James 5:16

The principle is clear enough. Anyone who wishes to find a clean heart and the peace that goes with it, and anyone who wishes to be healed, must confess what remains hidden. Without confession there is no healing.

Confession is not exclusively for our own sin; it can certainly include the effect of someone else's sin as it affects us in detrimental ways. We see this often in the Psalms, where the writer is weighed down by the sins of others in the way that they treated him. He still felt the need to talk to God about it before he found relief within himself.

When God counsels his hurting people, he gently leads them out of their denial. As a teacher who was deeply concerned about helping people, Jesus said, "If you hold to my teaching, you are really my disciples. Then you will know the truth, and the truth will set you free" (John 8:31–32). Jesus is describing a process of truth that can rescue anyone from the bondage of past abuse.[1]

Such is the survivor's task of confession. Find the problem. Admit it. Face the problem as one's own. Process what is found. Work through the feelings and memories, painful as that may be. Accept the truth of what has happened, for it is the discovery of truth that brings freedom. Then and only then is the survivor ready to take the next step—repairing the damage.

10

Facing the Enemy Within

Oh, how I love your law!
I meditate on it all day long.
Your commands make me wiser than my enemies,
for they are ever with me.
I have more insight than all my teachers,
for I meditate on your statutes.
I have more understanding than the elders,
for I obey your precepts.
I have kept my feet from every evil path
so that I might obey your word.
I have not departed from your laws,
for you yourself have taught me.
How sweet are your words to my taste,
sweeter than honey to my mouth!
I gain understanding from your precepts;
therefore I hate every wrong path.
Psalm 119:97–104

Once the problem has been found and faced, the next part of healing is to change the way life has been. Survivors are tired of living the way they are. Life has been a long, hard journey. Any constructive change would be a help. The biblical word for basic change in one's life is *repentance*. It literally means "a change of direction." "I was going the wrong way, but now I choose to go a different way." This doesn't necessarily mean survivors have great sins that need repentance, although they often feel that way. It does mean their life has not been going well at all. A major change in direction to something a lot more productive and satisfying is greatly needed.

Challenge Old Beliefs

Because of a lot of negative conditioning from their abusers, survivors of childhood sexual abuse have developed a lot of wrong beliefs about themselves and others. Many are firmly convinced they are ugly, worthless, unworthy of the attention of others, guilty and shameful beings, helpless, and unable to handle life. They see themselves as damaged goods, wounded and hurting. Their feelings are very strong and very real. Survivors believe these distorted ideas about themselves to be solid fact and will not be easily swayed. Attempts to make survivors think only good thoughts and ignore the negative will meet with only temporary success; eventually the old problems will come back.

Where do the self-concepts of ugliness, unworthiness, and self-hatred come from? What are their roots? Many survivors strongly believe the following thoughts:

1. The survivor believes that he or she is an awful, evil person for allowing the abuse to take place. "I should have put an end to this somehow. Why didn't I fight it off? Why didn't I just refuse? Nobody else stoops this low. I must be an awful person. I feel so ashamed of myself."

2. The survivor believes that he or she is unacceptable to others—ruined for life. "If anyone ever knew about this part of my life, they would certainly condemn and reject me. I am not good enough for others." Therefore, the survivor stays on the outer fringes socially. The survivor wants very much to be accepted

by others but is too afraid of rejection to venture the friendliness necessary for social acceptance.

3. The survivor believes that he or she is somehow a sinful, evil person because of the sexual urges. "I shouldn't have ever let myself feel this way. I don't understand why I sometimes actually felt some excitement and wanted more, even though I hated every minute. I have such a struggle with sexual urges. They frighten me. Nobody would want me around. I would be a bad influence."

4. The survivor struggles with a lot of inner anger that impacts his or her whole life. The anger is usually kept under the surface in the form of depression, smoldering personality, or frequent explosions out of proportion to the real problem at hand. "I feel anger toward everyone. I don't understand where all this anger comes from. Nobody wants to be around an angry person, so who would want to be around me? Why can't I handle situations like others do?"

5. The survivor feels very vulnerable. He or she is afraid of being hurt again and therefore keeps a high wall around self. To let others see his or her inner feelings is too dangerous. Therefore, the survivor must keep a safe distance from others either by emotional aloofness or by a wall of hostility that makes the person hard to reach or unapproachable. "Those I loved have hurt me so much, I believe others could do the same again if I gave them the chance. I won't let anyone get close to me; that way I won't have to feel that awful pain again."

Each one of us has developed an underlying belief system about ourselves and the world around us based on our life's experience. Although we don't consciously think these beliefs out loud, our reactions and behavior are very much controlled by them. Not all of these beliefs are helpful, and not all of them bring about the behavior we would like. Recognizing and then changing faulty beliefs is similar to the process of the renewing of the mind, which in turn transforms our lives and behavior (see Rom. 12:2).

Correct the Myths

Every belief needs to fit facts and reality, whether fully understood or not. Let's take a look at the myths that many survivors believe and check them with the facts. Then adjustments in the beliefs can be made where appropriate.

> MYTH: "I must be evil for allowing the abuse to take place. I should have stopped it somehow."
> FACT: A young child is in no position to fight off an adult.

Initially this is hard for the survivor to grasp. I often ask the question, "If you learned that your five-year-old child had been sexually abused by an adult, would you blame the child?" The answer invariably comes back, "No, of course not, I would feel sorry for the child and angry at the abuser." And I reply, "Of course. Then why do you blame yourself? How are you different from that child?"

By stepping back to look beyond self to the same experience in another, the survivor is able to absorb the fact that the abuser was much larger, much stronger, and much more able to overpower the victim. Whether by brute force or by clever persuasion and seduction, the abuser violates the trust and dependency of the child. Deliverance comes when the survivor comes to realize that *the abuser must take the responsibility for the abuse, not the helpless child!*

One of the hardest tasks of all is for survivors to forgive themselves. To come to grips with the fact that they let this awful stuff happen again and again is too much to handle. But as survivors let the facts sink in, they begin to see for the first time how much their trust was betrayed, how vulnerable they really were, and how overpowering the situation really was. The abuser was usually several times the size of the child and was usually someone the child already knew and trusted. Survivors must then come to realize that they were set up by the abuser. Not a happy thought, but true.

> MYTH: "I am not good enough for others to accept. They would reject me if they knew enough about me. I am ugly, dumb, stupid, a misfit. I am different from everyone else—unacceptable."
>
> FACT: An abused child is a worthwhile human being who, unfortunately, has been brainwashed to believe a lie about his or her self-worth.

Abused children have been treated as though they are somewhat less than human. They have been put in the position of being someone's object of conquest and pleasure, a possession, a sex slave to someone who has badly mistreated them. Often they have been brutalized, humiliated, shamed, blamed as being worse than the abuser for being a part of the whole thing. They are often told that no one would want them after this.

The child's own developmental need for love, affirmation, a sense of importance, respect, and safety are short-circuited. The normal, happy times of childhood are ruined and destroyed. If the parent, who should be the child's protector, does not believe the victim or blames the victim, the harm is even greater. The child is treated differently from other children and therefore believes that he or she is different.

The survivor must begin to see that he or she has been *brainwashed to believe a lie.* Further deliverance comes when the survivor realizes the real truth to be, "Abuse does not ruin me for life. I am a worthwhile human being!"

MYTH: "The fact that I struggle with sexual urges demonstrates that I am a sinful, evil person, and therefore people wouldn't want to be around me."

FACT: Everyone has sexual urges; God made us that way. The real problem is not an evil child but it is an evil abuser who knows how to manipulate the child and to cause sexual arousal without the child's understanding, consent, or participation.

An abuser who is much older knows how to stimulate a child, to awaken sexual urges and desires long before their time by touch and stimulation in genital areas. The child doesn't know what is really happening, only that the child's own sexual arousal is activated. The child can readily believe he or she is somehow initiating it. Many times the abuser will then blame the child for "wanting to do this" and therefore inflicts even more guilt and shame. The fact that others try to blame the victim for what happened adds to the whole abuse as well. Major guilt and distorted thinking arise out of this kind of thought process.

Many survivors will still feel guilt over their excitement as well as their willingness to go along with the abuse even though they hated it at the same time. But sex is exciting; God made it that way. If sex were boring, most of us wouldn't have been born. Too much bother. Again, the excitement and sexual arousal are only natural responses. The child's abuser purposely stimulates the child as a way of enticing the child to repeatedly submit to the abuse, all for the abuser's satisfaction. The child's feelings or needs are not even taken into account by the abuser. The child is little more than an *object* to the perpetrator.

Deliverance comes as the survivor understands *the self-centered intent of the abuser, and the fact that the child's sexual response came from the abuser's purposeful manipulation of an innocent mind.* The real sense of blame can then be shifted away from self to the adult abuser who was acting out of greed, power, and lust.

> MYTH: "I have so much anger inside of me. Nobody could love me as I am. Certainly God could never accept me like this. I can't seem to stop the anger from bubbling out and ruining things. I always feel so bad afterwards."
>
> FACT: Anger has an origin and a just cause. Not all anger is wrong. Anger is quite appropriate when there is injustice, unfairness, and manipulation.

Note the anger demonstrated by Jesus at those who had made a lucrative and highly profitable business within God's house of worship by selling "approved" animals for sacrifice and all the other details necessary for "appropriate" worship at the temple at Jerusalem. They were ripping off everyone and lining their own pockets with their greed. Jesus drove them out, saying that God intended this to be a house of prayer, but they had made it a den of thieves (Mark 11:15–17). I would have loved to have been there, to see the confusion, animals running loose, money scattered around, the corrupt dealers scurrying to minimize their losses. I am sure many people talked about the scene for weeks after, rejoicing that the longtime abuses at God's house were being addressed.

Or consider the time Jesus told off the Pharisees—the powerful religious leaders of the day. His blast of fury came near the end of his ministry on earth, after three years of their constant badgering, trickery, and condemnation. Enough was enough. They were supposedly the representatives of everything that was holy and right. But instead of bringing a message of good news to the people, they added to the already heavy burdens of the people by endless regulations and rules to be kept in order to be right before God. Yes, guilt trips were very much alive back then too. Worship had to be in certain exact ways, or it was not acceptable. Everything the Pharisees did was to call attention to themselves. They invented all kinds of loopholes to escape responsibility under the guise of religiosity. Jesus called them names, can you imagine? "Hypocrites, blind guides, blind fools, whitewashed graves, a brood of vipers!" (see Matthew 23). Wow! Where was all this anger coming from? The Pharisees had developed an abusive system with themselves in the seat of power. They used the tools of guilt, humiliation, overwhelming requirements, and endless rules to debilitate the people. Jesus' anger was appropriate to the situation.

The purpose of the abuser is the same: to empower himself or herself at the expense of another. The survivor of childhood sexual abuse has suffered much at the hands of a more powerful adult. Anger felt toward the abuser is appropriate. The survivor *should* feel some realistic anger, because the anger has a real and just cause. But anger kept inside becomes depression or may show up as physical ailments that are stress related, and letting anger fly without control will cause overreactions, and others may get hurt in the process.

So how can the anger be released? A helpful way to view anger may be found in seeing anger as a warning signal, like the flashing red lights at a railroad crossing. They are signals telling us that danger is ahead—stop, look, and listen. The feeling of anger tells us the same. *Anger alerts us to a problem.* If someone is trying to make me feel guilty when that is not appropriate, anger rises within. If someone is trying to manipulate me to do something that is not really within my standards of right and wrong, good or bad, anger should rise up from within as a warning signal. I need to stop, look, and listen to what is happening. A look at the following diagram may help us to understand a constructive way of dealing with anger, or any potentially destructive feelings for that matter.

An unfair or abusive situation first impacts us on a *feeling* level. The anger we might feel on the inside tells us

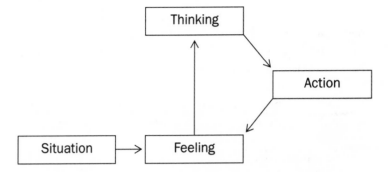

something about what is happening. The feelings give us an early warning system, like flashing red lights telling us to stop, look, and listen. Something is wrong. From there, we go to *thinking,* where we sort out what is happening and possible ways of dealing with the problem. Once we have thought through the problem and worked out a possible solution, we must go on to *action* in most cases. The action needs to be appropriate to the situation, but we must do whatever we can to resolve a problem. We cannot ignore it. Once appropriate action has been taken, the feelings fade, because there is no longer fuel for the fire. The problem is basically resolved.

Note that the early warning signal of the problem comes at a *feeling* level. Acting on the feeling, however, may not bring good results. Punching someone in the face goes straight from *feeling* to *action,* but it probably would not bring an acceptable solution to the problem. Doing nothing brings no desirable results either, just a dangling feeling of anger that can slip into depression. The missing step is *thinking.* The feeling identifies the source of the problem. Thinking now must take over to figure out what must be done about a problem. Responsible action must then follow. Ignoring appropriate action keeps us stuck in the same problem that created the anger in the first place.

An important point: the energy of anger can be channeled into *determination* to take whatever necessary *action* appropriate to the situation. When we have done everything we can constructively do about a situation, we are then able to put it behind us and move on to happier pursuits. That's a *positive use of anger*. Don't be afraid of it. Determination can take us a long way in overcoming entanglements of our past.

Sometimes the anger is so overwhelming, we are afraid to do anything with it for fear of losing self-control and hurting someone or ourselves. We may need ways to cool down the anger before we can channel it constructively. There are things that help:

- *Physical exercise* such as a long, brisk walk, vigorously chopping wood, cleaning house like a whirlwind, or a heavy workout can clear our minds and help release some of the anger.
- *Listening to music* can "soothe the wild beast" inside.
- *Writing* the angry feelings on a paper that will later be crumpled up and destroyed also can help.
- *Ventilating* with a friend may help take some steam off, but there must be a clear understanding with the friend just what you are doing so that the anger is not taken personally, and keep in mind that too much ventilation can also increase the anger.

Remember, the whole purpose of following any of these suggestions is to *resolve* the anger, not just express it.

Deliverance from the deep well of anger within is not found in self-condemnation but in *understanding the anger has a legitimate cause, finding a safe release of anger in appropriate ways, and channeling its energy into determination*. Anger can thus become useful in energizing us to work out what needs to be resolved.

MYTH: "If I let people know how I really feel, I will get hurt. I can't afford to let anyone get close to me; it's too painful."

FACT: While it is true that none of us can afford to share with everyone the deepest secrets of our hearts, we cannot afford to be loners either. None of us can really stand by ourselves for great lengths of time, and this is especially true for survivors of abuse.

It is important to learn to share our inner selves with a few select friends we have cultivated over time. When two people are committed to each other as friends, there is something about sharing their inner selves that enriches both lives, drawing them together in a common bond of deeper friendship and appreciation of each other. The one who does the sharing is enriched by the fact that he or she has ventured into a new area of friendship never before experienced, all because of a willingness to become vulnerable. Instead of being rejected or mocked, the sharer is received with warmth, understanding, and an increased closeness. A rewarding experience! Old fears of rejection begin to fade away; vulnerability has given way to new strength and confidence! It is tremendous for the survivor to have a nonthreatening, normal relationship that can prosper and grow, born out of openness instead of defensiveness. Such a friendship can be a healing experience. Deliverance for the survivor, then, comes from *venturing out from behind one's protective wall to one or two trustworthy friends, and both are enriched together.*

MYTH: "If I let myself feel any of this deep, inward pain, I will be overwhelmed, and never be able to get it back into control again. I will become a basket case."

FACT: Generally, our mind does not let us view more than we can handle at one time. Our well-developed defenses take over so that once the survivor has worked through a portion of a memory, the rest shuts off until the time he or she is ready to work through some more.

If the survivor is in therapy with someone well trained in helping dig out the memories, the therapist takes the responsibility for pacing the sessions. The therapist can slow the process down whenever necessary.

Working through the pain is a necessary part of the therapy. All of us wish there were an easier way, therapists and survivors alike. No helping person likes to see another in pain. Some will object at this point and say, "You just need to turn it over to God, and he will take the pain away." The difference lies in what we each mean by that statement. Clearly God is interested in our growth and is very much a part of our growing process throughout our lifetime. The apostle Paul wrote, "Being confident of this, that he who began a good work in you will carry it on to completion until the day of Christ Jesus" (Phil. 1:6). But how will this growth take place? Will God miraculously remove the memories, the pain and anguish, the fear, and the self-hatred? God can. But he usually ministers to our growth through other people.

To those who say, "God took it all away," I would say, "You can be very thankful." That has not been my experience or that of the multitude of others I have known. In most areas of life, pain comes before healing. I would also ask the person who says God has taken away all the pain to be very sure he or she has not simply used the defense of denial and intellectualization, thus burying the hurt deeper. Time will certainly tell. If depression and anxiety return, the person needs to search more deeply, until he or she discovers the truth.

We must not lose sight of the fact that childhood sexual abuse causes severe damage to the child in the early formative years and sabotages basic milestones of emotional development that are essential to becoming a normal adult. No simplistic treatment is going to fill the horrendous gaps of emotional development, the emptiness, the pain of childhood betrayal of trust, or the extensive destruction of self-worth that has taken place. Major reconstruction is required. That takes time. Deliverance for the survivor, then, comes not through a loss of self-control, but through a *careful and deliberate process of working through the pain a step at a time, which in turn brings healing.*

MYTH: "God could never accept me because of the way my life has been. I am too evil."

FACT: The fact of the matter is that God cannot accept *any* of us because of the way our life has been. All of us are sinners and have come far short of God's righteousness. But the cross of Christ made it all possible: Salvation, forgiveness, and acceptance come as a *gift* from God, not something we earn (see Eph. 2:8–9).

Acceptance from God has nothing to do with how good or bad one person is compared to another. God reaches out in love to each of us. Anyone who is willing to reach back can accept his gift of forgiveness by faith in the finished work of Christ.

Deliverance for the survivor comes from accepting that fact: No matter how bad any of us feel about ourselves or what we think we have done, *the cross of Christ is sufficient to cover all our sins, and God's love reaches to anyone who is willing to accept his gift.*

Realizing God's Love

Most survivors of abuse have real difficulty accepting God's love. First, they believe they are too unlovable. Second, they have problems relating to a God they cannot see when love by those they can see has been very distorted. Third, they have problems believing God really cares. "After all," many reason, "if God really loved me, why would he have allowed all of this to happen in the first place? How could a God of love let me suffer such horrendous pain as a little child?" A valid question, and, admittedly, a difficult one to adequately answer. Let me speak to part of the question now:

1. Trust in God, who is far away and seemingly un-
reachable, will not become real for most survivors
until they have experienced solid acceptance, sincere
caring, responsible and trustworthy action, and sensitivity to their feelings on a human level. For therapy
to be effective, all of these characteristics must be
present. A close relationship with a confidential
friend who demonstrates these characteristics also
helps considerably. The survivor will test the sincerity of the therapist or friend again and again. Each
test of caring successfully passed develops increased
trust and growth in the survivor and shortens the
long bridge to relating to God who seems far off. But
until the survivor has experienced genuine caring on
a human level, he or she will find it hard to relate to
pure love from God on a spiritual level.

2. I am not sure why God takes the rap for all the evil
things that happen in the world. God does not orig-
inate evil. But we say, "Couldn't God prevent all the
wrong things from happening in the world?" He
could, but he has chosen to hold that off until the day
of judgment. People abuse other people because of
greed, lust, and the need for power, not because God
put them up to it. The abuse continues in a large
measure because people cover their actions, or others allow it to continue by reason of their own need
for denial. Certainly a lot more sensitivity toward innocent victims along with swift and sure justice
could help to reduce the amount of abuse. But as
long as there are evil people in this world, we will
have abuse and abusers. Only when God removes all
evil from the world will all this stop permanently.
That time is yet to come. God never promised to deliver us from all evil in this present world. He did
promise to be with us when it happens, to help us
through it (John 16:33).

3. The survivor may not realize that God's own sorrow for what has happened is deep and profound. The fact that God did not directly stop the abuse does not reflect his lack of interest and love. When God restrains his wrath against evil and delays his final judgment, God actually hurts, as in the anguish of childbirth, writhing in pain for the right moment to carry out judgment and justice (Isa. 42:14).[1]

4. Survivors should realize that Jesus Christ was also a victim. He suffered unimaginable pain. He knew what it meant to bear the shame of others. He knew what it meant to be alone, naked, bleeding in the darkness as he pathetically cried out, "My God, my God, why have you forsaken me?" (Mark 15:34). No one better understands what it means to suffer under the weight of someone else's sin. No one better understands what it means to suffer in the darkness while God and all the angels of heaven remained silent.[2]

Infinite good came out of that terrible abuse and darkness. Christ used his suffering to bring millions of people into an eternal relationship with the Father. His suffering showed that as the Father comforted Jesus, so the Father can comfort us.[3]

Marjorie struggled with the age-old question as well: "If God really loved me, why did he allow all this to happen?" As she wrestled with the question, she had a very vivid dream. The dream took her to the woods—the familiar place where her stepfather forced her under threat of death to have sex with him. As she watched from a distance, she saw the abuse taking place in her dream as though in real life. She was troubled and fearful. Where was God in all this? Suddenly a bright figure dressed in shining white stood before her. She was startled and a bit frightened but perceived this to be an angel from God. The heavenly messenger simply said, "It will turn out all right." The messenger disappeared, and the dream ended, but Marjorie now had peace that it would indeed work out in the end in spite of her suffering. And it did. She got the help she needed to rebuild her life and move on to a promising career.

I don't know all the answers to this nagging question as to why God allows all this suffering to happen. I do know that a survivor can be healed from the traumas of the past, can move on to a productive life, and can come out a stronger person in spite of it all. Healing is available from the God who understands.

Healing for DID and SRA

The process of healing for Dissociative Identity Disorder and Satanic Ritual Abuse survivors is much more complicated. The memories of their abuse are so far removed from conscious awareness that they are hard to access by ordinary methods. Only little bits and pieces can be retrieved—not enough to make any real sense out of all the confusion and strange things happening in the survivor's life.

Memories of severe abuse before age six are more deeply hidden. It is believed that the frontal part of the brain is not yet fully developed before that age, and consequently a child does not retain memory in the same way at younger ages. Thus normal recall of events seems to be walled off beyond the usual layers of the unconscious memory. One approach that works with DID and SRA is teaching the survivor a deeper form of relaxation in order to access the hidden memories. The person is helped to find the state somewhere between conscious thought and sleep, where the body is at rest, the distractions of the outside world are shut out, and the person is able to look deeper into the mind and search out its buried secrets.

It is important to remember that deep relaxation has no other purpose than to help access memories. The use of hypnotic suggestion or manipulation or the planting of ideas in the survivor's mind has no place here and can in itself become abusive to a vulnerable survivor. The survivor must be given the control of the process, and it must be made very clear that the survivor can come out of this state at any time there is something too threatening or unwanted. *The therapist must exercise integrity and full respect for the person and rights of the survivor.*

> After becoming very relaxed, Betty would picture herself in an elevator, going down, down, even below the basement. She would get off the elevator and enter a large room, something like a parlor of a house. Off of this room was a long hallway with a number of doors—each a room where a personality lived. Usually one of the personalities was in the parlor when she arrived, and that particular alter would tell her part of the story as she remembered it. Another time, a different alter would appear.
>
> Each alter was different from the others, and though in the body of an adult, each acted the age Betty had been at the time that alter was formed. Some alters only had feelings they felt intensely but had no idea of their origin. Others had parts of memories of events they could not connect together. None of them initially acknowledged the existence of others as being from the same person; they were all strangers to one another. As the process of discovering memory went on, the alters became more acquainted with each other, could begin to piece together parts of memories into a greater whole, and thus learned to communicate together.
>
> Jill found her relaxation in visualizing a large field of flowers beneath a blue sky and fluffy clouds. As she wandered about this pleasant place, she found new persons appearing, each with different characteristics, each with a specified task. She found many small children alters, most from ages three to five—some angry, some rather

lost, some in shock, some extremely small and frightened, some very lonely, some in pain. She discovered alters who were helpful, and a few who were frightening.

At first it was hard for Jill to see that these alters were all
expressions of herself at different points in her life and her
abuse. In the course of her therapy, she recognized herself
in some of the alters that matched childhood photographs.
As we continued on, she found more and more childhood alters, indicating a great deal of abuse at very young ages. For
a while there seemed to be an endless supply of alters. Gradually the pieces of her abuse fit together, and she could describe some sections from beginning to end.

When one of the child alters was present, the memories were very real, just like it was all happening right
now. When she would return to her host personality, the
one who dealt with present everyday life, the memories
seemed so far away and unreal. That is how dissociation
works to protect the survivor from the trauma of the
childhood experiences.

Jill noticed, however, that painful as the memories
were, the more she pieced them together and the more
she was able to correct the accompanying distorted
thinking, the stronger she became as a person. Her energy level increased, her courage to handle the difficult
things in life improved, her self-confidence grew, her
level of anxiety and depression decreased considerably.
The task was not yet complete, but healing was taking
place. Eventually health would be found in the joining of
separated alters into one whole person.

For very complicated Dissociative Identity Disorder survivors, an alternative goal is to get to the point where all of
the personalities work together as a unified whole. Living a
normal life would be a tremendous step forward.

The healing of Satanic Ritual Abuse survivors is very similar to Dissociative Identity Disorder in that most have multiple personalities induced by their abusers to prevent them

from remembering the atrocities that followed. One important difference, however, is that SRA survivors' problems may include demonic influence, oppression, or programming. Although some will argue against the existence of such demonic powers, and still others are ready to find demons in every imaginable place, I tend to take the reporting and perceived experience of the SRA survivor as it comes. I handle their memories and visualization with care, because it is very real to them. I also try to avoid "leading the witness," that is, putting ideas into the survivors' mind to produce a desired conclusion. The therapist must be open-minded enough to help SRA survivors work through the truth of what is there but objective enough to avoid conclusions that are unwarranted and based on speculation.

There will be times when the principles of spiritual warfare may need to be applied. The therapist may find a need to bind a demon or order a demon to leave the survivor, to cease its oppression. Since demons are more powerful than humans, the act of silencing or casting out demons can only be done on the authority of God, the power of the blood of Christ, and the energy of the Holy Spirit. But again, do not oversimplify the problem. Simply casting out demons will not in and of itself heal an SRA survivor. There are still many nondemonic alters as a result of the terrible and barbaric abuse that will need healing and many difficult memories to be worked through. That process may take a long time.

Care should be taken to not confuse destructive alters with demons. Most DID survivors have a very frightening alter whose task is to protect the system from perceived danger, and it can appear to be very bizarre and threatening. To ascribe a demonic state to a destructive or persecutor alter that is not demonic only serves to drive the alter deeper and to unbalance the system.[4]

Further help can be found from a group of Christian people praying for both the survivor and the therapist. Likewise, physical protection for the survivor may be necessary. Other coven members may well attempt to find the survivor and punish him or her for revealing secret information. SRA survivors may be programmed to harm, mutilate, or even kill themselves if they reveal information, and thus precautions must be taken to protect the survivor. Many do become suicidal. Harm also may come to the therapist. This is not for the weak in faith.

Herb had only limited memories of his past. He came from a very confused home background. He recalled a very difficult and emotionally abusive father, a few memory fragments of sexual abuse as a child by someone yet unknown, some vague memories of people in black, hooded cloaks with candles gathered around in a circle, and other minor fragments. He recalled having a great interest in learning about witchcraft as a child.

Herb's present experience included a lot of days in which he seemed to be struggling against unseen forces he could not explain. He had a repeated picture in his mind of an ugly creature with claws or talons tightly dug into his leg. Whenever we talked of any of this, his right arm would go cold or numb, the arm that "did the deed," as he explained it.

Herb had repeated mental pictures of auto accidents. He then experienced two accidents just as he had pictured within a few months of each other. Both cars were totaled, but he was safe. I had one minor accident myself, and several close calls in quick succession. From that time on, a group of Christians was asked to pray for his safety as well as mine, and the problem of accidents went away.

As we worked together in therapy, suddenly a clear picture of many creatures something like bats or locusts coming from behind and entering into him flashed into his mind. It was like a memory of being invaded by evil spirits. He also had some clear dreams of a group of hooded persons gathered around a large table in a barn, and one woman with nothing but a robe over her. He had a related dream of being forced against his will to drink blood. I showed him a drawing made by an SRA survivor of a black mass. Herb was stunned and upset, for that was exactly what he was visualizing.

Efforts to access further information and memories were often blocked, and we got nothing. Attempts to identify a specific demon seemed to go nowhere. One day as we again experienced blockage, I simply said, "If there is someone inside who is blocking further information, I bind you in the name of Jesus." Immediately Herb had a flashback of his sexual abuse as a child. He sat there stunned for a few minutes as he realized what happened. He left lighthearted.

There was still a long way to go in Herb's healing process, but an important hurdle had been crossed. It was clear we were dealing with something unusual, but the power of God would guide us through and help us with the healing process.

DID and SRA people are usually very intelligent, creative, and talented people. They have a great potential as they are helped to gather the various alter fragments of themselves together into one whole person. For them, the pain of the awful memories becomes worth it in order to find healing and be all that they can be.

Summary

Vital to healing from the extensive damage of childhood sexual abuse is the process of challenging old beliefs, feelings, and distorted images that need to be corrected. This will happen as the survivor faces each of these distortions of thoughts and feelings, examines each one in the light of reality and the truth of the Word of God, and consciously makes choices to put aside the old and think new thoughts that are solidly based. As the survivor learns to think realistic and positive thoughts about self-worth and value, his or her behavior will change to fit the new belief system. The confusion fades; healing takes place. The survivor now experiences normal thought patterns and normal experiences. A much healthier view of God's love begins to shine through at this point, and inner renewal can begin to take place.

11

Facing the Enemy Outside

Cast your cares on the LORD
and he will sustain you;
he will never let the righteous fall.
But you, O God, will bring down the wicked
into the pit of corruption;
bloodthirsty and deceitful men
will not live out half their days.
But as for me, I trust in you.
                                    Psalm 55:22–23

Not only is there a lot of healing that must take place within the individual, but a lot must also happen on the outside in relationships with others.

Confusion in Relationships

The severe betrayal of trust that takes place during childhood sexual abuse leaves the child survivor confused about relationships long into adulthood, unable to know if anyone can be trusted. Once the underlying fear of being manipulated or taken advantage of has taken hold, the survivor remains on guard, particularly with aggressive, controlling persons. The hard lessons of early experience are not easily left behind even though the actual abuse itself is now past. The underlying fear of being overpowered by others remains intact.

Many survivors will shy away from aggressive people. Because of a need to be accepted and liked, survivors will find themselves trying to do many things to make other people happy at the expense of their own self-worth. Survivors may try even harder with an aggressive and less accepting recipient, thus creating a painful relationship where acceptance is never found no matter how great the effort. Or some survivors may take the opposite track and become aggressive themselves in order to ward off other threatening individuals. None of these strategies really work well over the years. Each has its own problems. Each brings diminishing rewards and increasing difficulties.

Insecurity in relationships likewise shows up as discomfort with people who are the same sex as the abuser. A male child abused by a male will have confused and uneasy relationships with other males and may have problems feeling adequate as a male. A female child abused by a male will have discomfort with men, particularly with aggressive or seductive ones. A male child abused by a female will have confusion and difficulty with other females and may have a strong need to be in control in most situations involving females.

The first step of the healing process in relationships with others comes from the changes within the inner self. The survivor must begin to change the wrong beliefs and feelings about other people and begin to realize that other people are not all dangerous. In fact, some of them can actually become supportive friends for the survivor if given the chance.

A second important step of healing is found in the willingness to *take definite steps to connect socially with other people, especially those of the same sex as the abuser.* Admittedly this will not be easy. However, the failure to do so will only result in further alienation. No survivor can afford to shut off half of the population of the world simply because of the gender of his or her abuser.

The survivor will be tempted to say, "Look, I have struggled enough in life. Do I have to work at this too? They should understand that I hurt too much inside." The answer is a resounding, "Yes! You do have to make the effort." Unless survivors work at cultivating friends and social relationships, they will be badly misunderstood and will further isolate themselves, which they cannot afford to do. All of us need to be able to relate to others, for none of us can stand completely on our own. The task is too great.

The old proverb stands true: "If a person would have friends, he must show himself friendly." Survivors cannot expect others to understand their reluctance in relationships unless they are willing to share something of themselves. If a survivor is able to share with a trusted friend of the same gender as his or her abuser and experience acceptance, it can melt away a lot of the fears.

> As a survivor, I had been uncomfortable with other males. Back in the days when my own abuse occurred, no one ever spoke of such matters. Although I was a reasonably intelligent and capable person, I never felt adequate or comfortable with other males. I found it much easier on a social level to relate to females. I could talk easily with women but not with men. I was often unsure how to take male roles with any degree of confidence. I studied how other males did things, never being quite sure of what was really normal. My discomfort went on for years.
>
> Finally, I shared something of my own abuse with another trustworthy male and received caring and affirmation. Surprise! A strange thing happened—a lot of the fear and inadequacy faded away. The spell had been broken. I felt free to relate to other males as well. Even more freedom followed. I saw a shift taking place from identification with females to identification with males. I am now able to relate to both with reasonable confidence.

> Joe realized he had a real problem with authority figures. He was always tense around them, always fearing the worst, expecting to be taken advantage of. It had cer-

tainly happened enough times to warrant some fear. Joe had often reacted inwardly with anger and inner rebellion. Eventually, however, he began to realize that he left himself wide open by being too timid and apprehensive.

Joe finally grew very tired of the old defeating patterns. Instead of just keeping his opinions to himself, he began to speak up, looking for holes in the conversation to get in a word. At first others did not seem to notice that much, but once he made his points clear and others could see the validity to what he was saying, he received an increased audience and greater respect. Self-confidence grew. He tried new things he would never have attempted before. The old fears did not have the same power anymore. The old victim image was fading away, and the walls of protection were coming down. New growth and healing were taking place. Ideas that were only dreams and longings were now beginning to become realities. Life had become a lot more fulfilling.

Sexual Confusion

Another very important area of confusion has to do with the normal expression of sexuality, which is very much a part of each one of us. The problem shows up in two basic areas:

1. interpersonal boundaries
2. normal sexual expression within marriage

Where is the normal expression of sexuality appropriate, and where is it not? This question may not be a problem for a lot of people, but because the survivor of childhood sexual abuse has been violated at a young age by a trusted person, both the normal boundaries of sexual expression and its appropriateness have been shattered. The power of sex has been set in motion long before its time. The boundaries of who is an appropriate sexual partner and when sexual activity is okay have already been overturned. Sex and love

are garbled together. Most survivors will have sexual esca-
pades they may well regret in their older but wiser years.
Some will be in a desperate search for love by sexual en-
counters with many partners. Many will live out the early
sexual experiences of their abuse with another, but this time
being the one who is in control. Sexual self-control will be
difficult. Few will escape confusion in finding appropriate
sexual boundaries.

The sense of appropriate sexual expression in marriage
takes a while to get sorted out. Most survivors search for
answers as to what really is normal. They learn a lot by trial
and error, that is, a lot of trial and a number of errors. They
begin to put together a better way and make more constructive choices about what to do with all the external stimulation and influence around them. Many decide to reserve this
for marriage and someone who really cares.

Males who have been abused by males may have somewhat less difficulty expressing their sexuality in marriage.
A male-female relationship will certainly be more natural
to them than male to male. Though many male survivors
fear homosexuality developing in their lives, the majority
are not drawn to that kind of lifestyle. Most are glad to be
free from anything similar to their abuse. The bigger problem is that of *containing* their own sexuality, as their sexual
desire tends to be hyped up at a very young age. Careful
choices in marriage can help greatly. Finding a loving wife
who also enjoys sexual expression can be very helpful.
Keeping open communication and accountability with that
wife as to inner struggles with sexual desire and attractions
can likewise be very helpful in strengthening both the male
survivor and the marriage. Learning to shake loose from
the associations of sex as power, shame, or anger will take
some time.

Women who have been abused by an older male may
well have more difficulty in the sexual relationship of marriage. In the past, male-to-female sex has been abusive, ex-

ploitative, and controlling—certainly anything but love. *The change from sex as an expression of exploitation to sex as an expression of love is a major shift and adjustment.* At first, sex in marriage may not be a problem, as the message deep down was that sex was a way to attract and get attention from a man. After a while, however, a wife has a deep need to know that she is loved for more than her body. She may then withhold sex, to see if her husband will love her in other ways. Since men tend to express a lot of their feelings through sex in marriage, the husband may not understand what is going on. He may well interpret her test of caring as personal rejection.

In other cases, the wife may be unable to separate her husband from her abuser in their sexual relationship. She may become very emotional, anxious, upset, and unable to complete the act. She may recoil at being touched in certain areas, become disgusted, or shut down emotionally and physically. Her husband will have great difficulty understanding. A lot of deeper healing work to unravel the confusion between sex and love, abuser and husband, may have to be done for the wife to adequately relate to her husband in their sexual relationship. Professional help may well be needed if there is any severity to the problem. The survivor will need to learn to forgive herself for whatever inappropriate experiences there have been in the past, as well as work through the inevitable confusion that results from childhood sexual abuse.

Can a survivor be helped by a therapist of the same gender as the abuser? Ideally therapists of both genders would work with a survivor. True, a female victimized by a male may have a harder time relating to a male therapist as she works through the issues of the abuse itself. Some of the issues may be very embarrassing, some will be too threatening. Trust is a major problem. However, if she can overcome those hurdles and get to the point where she can learn to safely relate to a male therapist who is accepting and kind, she could find major help in breaking through her wall of mistrust of men. She could then begin to separate her abuser from other males, and thus find it possible to build a good marriage. The same idea would be true with a male who has been abused by a female, and the use of a female therapist. There is also the issue of the survivor harboring a lot of anger toward the gender of the child's caretaker who failed to protect the child—another area needing healing. If having both male and female therapists is not possible, a confidential friend of the same sex can be very helpful. The interaction of support groups can be very useful in this area also.

Confrontation of Abusers

One very knotty problem has to do with confrontation of abusers. Opinions vary widely. Some believe that the survivor should go to his or her abuser as soon as possible and confront the person. Some believe this is a direct command from Scripture (see Matt. 18:15–17). There are problems with this, however. Some survivors would go with vengeance and hatred in their hearts. Some would even kill if they had the chance. Others would find confrontation much too dangerous, frightening, and threatening and would never attempt it.

I firmly believe that *confrontation must be handled with a great deal of care.* The survivor must be ready, the approach very carefully planned with a therapist, and the meeting handled very discreetly with a full knowledge of its expected effects. There are some who have rushed in with only very limited memory information of what really happened, have been full of anger, and have confronted a family member with no regard to how their accusations affect other family members. Sometimes the facts of what happened are not well enough in hand, and false accusations are made with resulting upheaval for everyone. A lot of unnecessary harm can be done without careful preparation.

There is something to be said for confrontation where that is possible. The act of confrontation can change the power structure of the once abusive relationship. If the survivor is able to successfully confront the abuser, get his or her point across, and leave without the need to make a hasty exit, a lot can be accomplished. In this case, the former victim has now taken charge, and the power issue is broken. But not all turn out this well. In some cases the survivor makes the attempt to confront the abuser, only to become again intimidated by the abuser who may laugh in the victim's face. In this case, nothing positive has been accomplished. The survivor was not yet strong enough for such a step and again feels like a defeated victim at the mercy of the abuser.

A lot of healing has to take place before considering the step of confrontation. The memories must first be well worked through so that they are no longer frightening. The feelings of anger, guilt, shame, and fear and the depths of the hurt must first be dealt with before a proper confrontation can effectively take place. Until a lot of healing work is done, the survivor is not likely to be strong enough to attempt something as difficult as confronting his or her abuser.

Keep in mind also that the biblical guidelines warn against seeking revenge: "Do not take revenge, my friends, but leave room for God's wrath, for it is written: 'It is mine to avenge; I will repay,' says the Lord" (Rom. 12:19). The real purpose of confrontation is to correct a serious problem and to restore a seriously fractured relationship where that may be possible. The Scriptures also say, "Brothers, if someone is caught in a sin, you who are spiritual should restore him gently. But watch yourself, or you also may be tempted" (Gal. 6:1). Restoration may not be quite what we had in mind in confrontation, but until we have come to that mind-set, confrontation could become potentially explosive and may do more harm than good.

As a child, Marjorie had suffered extensive abuse from her stepfather. When she reached her late teens, she realized that he was now approaching her younger sister. Marjorie's anger burned. It was one thing to abuse her, but it was quite another for him to abuse her younger sister who had fewer defenses than she herself did.

Confrontation with the stepfather about his actions did no good, as he only laughed it off and denied any involvement. The mother would not help but instead blamed Marjorie herself for doing something to cause the problem. So Marjorie mustered up the courage to talk to a respected teacher and report what had been happening. The teacher in turn contacted the proper authorities. The stepfather was arrested, convicted, and sentenced to prison.

Marjorie had hoped that her stepfather would face up to his problem and get counseling while in prison. He refused, saying that he had become a Christian and that everything was okay now. But he in no way evidenced any changes in attitude or willingness to face up to what he had done. His denial was still as persistent as ever. Marjorie could not accept his excuses and knew that nothing would be different when he got out of prison. She was afraid for the rest of the family.

When the time came for the stepfather's parole hearing, Marjorie, still a teenager, was there. She presented her well-documented reasons why he should not be paroled at that time. Her abuser remained in jail a while longer. Eventually, as the mother reflected on what really had been happening to her family and just what kind of person she had married, she finally refused to take the stepfather back into the family.

Marjorie acted once more. She filed a civil suit against the stepfather for damages, and the stepfather fled the state. The family was now safe from his intrusions and abuse. Marjorie's anger had motivated her to take action which in turn stopped a damaging cycle in her family, one that the mother had been unable to face herself. Marjorie's courage and careful planning paid off.

Forgiveness

"Do you mean to say I have to forgive the person who abused me and caused all this pain? I don't want to hear it! That would be asking too much!" Such are the feelings of a lot of survivors who have been abused and molested. Their anguish is too great, their pain is too deep to even think the thought. There is no question that ongoing anger and resentment, if never dealt with, produce bitterness, depression, and even physical illness. Bitterness eats from within and poisons the soul. There is no joy to be found in hanging on to an unforgiving spirit. It leads to nowhere.

On the other side are the pious ones who say that we must forgive without question anyone who has ever hurt us. They are quick to quote any of a number of Scriptures that teach the principle of forgiveness. For example, "Bear with each other and forgive whatever grievances you may have against one another. Forgive as the Lord forgave you" (Col. 3:13). I think we need to find out what forgiveness really means for the survivor of childhood sexual abuse before we can accept or reject the teaching as good or bad.

Forgiveness is not a simple act that causes all the fear, mistrust, and hurt to suddenly disappear. Many Christians mistakenly assume that forgiving someone who has hurt them means no longer feeling pain, anger, or a desire for revenge. Forgiveness does not mean that painful memories of the past are wiped away; nor does it mean that a desire for justice is ignored. Nor does the survivor cease feeling a deep sense of anger and hurt for what has happened. In fact, real forgiveness cannot even be considered until those who have been abused come out of the darkness of denial and begin to recognize the weight of the wrongs committed against them.[1] A major trust has been broken, and severe damage has been inflicted on an innocent child. A vital relationship has been shattered. The pieces will not be put together that easily. Shattered trust takes time to heal.

The survivor needs to come to the place where he or she has worked through the shame, anger, hurt, and confusion created by his or her abuse. The process of healing needs to come to the point where the survivor can now let go of those feelings and move on with life. The survivor's perspective needs to change from the point, "You ruined my life forever," to, "Yes, you caused me a lot of damage, but I can now by the grace of God move on with my life. I can now forgive you for causing me a great deal of harm, but you no longer have any power or control over me. I am free!" Forgiveness, then, is letting go of hatred and bitterness so that the passion of the gospel and the boldness of love can fill our hearts.[2]

Not all abusers are seeking forgiveness. Most of them are too encrusted in their own denial to admit there ever was a problem. Other members of the family may not want to ever have to face the awful truths of what happened and are quick to bury everything. Some families will want "easy forgiveness" so that the abuser will be able to escape the consequences of his or her own behavior, such as prison or family shame that comes from public knowledge. In such cases the survivor may be asked to just forgive and let this nightmare be over.

However, forgiveness does not mean cutting short the consequences of the abuser's shameful behavior. "Easy forgiveness" may only free the abuser to abuse others. It is a basic law of life that all actions have consequences—good or bad. Yes, even jail can be within the will of God for an abuser. Verbal protestations of repentance do not automatically circumvent justice and consequences for evil. The survivor may have a forgiving spirit and still allow the abuser to go to jail, for that is the law of the land and the order of society; it has little to do with forgiveness. The survivor may wish to see his or her abuser get help while in prison in a special program for sexual offenders. If the abuser is a family member, the family unit may possibly be restored as the offender shows the evidence of life change and the family is helped through the steps of healing. The concept of "one big, happy family again" is a nice ideal, a goal to work toward, but it is dependent on a great deal of realistically based healing for everyone.

Complete forgiveness will be difficult without genuine repentance and sincere change on the part of the abuser. A lot has to take place before the survivor can again feel at all comfortable in the presence of his or her former abuser. Indeed, many steps will need to be taken to insure the survivor's safety. Opening the probability of further abuse under the guise of forgiveness is not a risk worth taking. A lot of time may need to pass for the survivor to be old enough and courageous enough to be in the unprotected presence of the former abuser.

For some, forgiveness may be possible only from a distance. The shattered bridge of trust may never be fully restored. Forgiveness for some may be more in the form of coming to the place of acceptance of the abuse, letting go of the hatred for the abuser, leaving it all behind as healing takes place, and moving on with one's life. I think the ability to reach the goal of forgiveness varies greatly with the individual and the extent of the damage done. Those with minor damage will more easily reach full forgiveness; others may never in this lifetime be able to get to that point. Let none of us be quick to judge others until we have walked in their shoes.

Taking Charge of Your Life

A vital part of healing is that of taking healthy charge of your life events. No longer does a survivor of childhood sexual abuse need to remain a victim, subject to the whims of manipulative people. Most survivors will need help in becoming more assertive interpersonally and socially. Instead of tiptoeing through life hoping no one will notice, or living in fear that someone will again trap them in unpleasant situations, survivors must learn to speak out. Instead of just giving in when someone is threatening or pressuring, the survivor needs to muster up the courage to firmly refuse and not be so concerned about hurting the other person's feelings. Usually people who are trying to take advantage of others are thinking only of themselves and have little sensitivity to the person they try to manipulate. Therefore, being assertive is not likely to hurt their feelings but only to frustrate their plans, which may well need to be frustrated.

> Joe found it difficult to express himself. When in a group, he did not speak up or share his thoughts or feelings. He thought that no one was interested in what he had to say, and the views of others were more important than his own. He was constantly asked to do this or that, and he always felt obligated to do what was asked. Consequently, he found himself handling a very heavy load of responsibility. But Joe was used to that, and he always found a way to cram yet another task into his overloaded schedule. He sometimes became resentful at the amount of work that was piled on him, but he never knew what to do about it.
>
> Joe finally came to the realization that not everything that he was asked to do was a directive from above and that not all of these requests fit into what he felt called to do. With great difficulty and fear of repercussions, he began to refuse a few things. Surprise! No repercussions. He felt greatly relieved of a lot of unnecessary responsibility and became a much happier person. He began to feel a sense of control in his life, instead of life controlling him.
>
> Caroline was experiencing feelings of anxiety and a sense of being trapped with certain people. Different men on the job would make offers to come to her apartment and do things for her. Her anxiety would rise when she

heard this, and the feeling of being trapped would start to close in. She was afraid of what these men were really up to but was unsure just how to keep them all away.

Finally, Caroline recognized her underlying belief that she could never ask someone to leave her own premises. Now she could see what was happening: She was afraid of being trapped in her own apartment by one of these guys and being unable to defend herself because of her inability to ask the person to leave before something really went wrong. Once she realized the belief was all wrong and that she had a right to ask anyone to leave her property, the anxiety went away. Caroline felt free to say what needed to be said and thus stand up for herself in a way that would make others listen. Her deliverance came by assertive action.

Choosing Good Friends

Important to a survivor's health and recovery is his or her choice of friends. It may be that his or her friendships are not very healthy relationships. These friends tend to be people with a lot of problems who have few if any other friends. They call or drop in and proceed to pour out a long litany of the same woes over and over that could vex the soul of the most patient counselor. They expect the survivor to solve their problems for them. They may do little to help themselves. Some of these friends are users, people who just take and take and give little in return. They will drain the survivor's resources, and in return give only the gift of guilt for not giving them more.

The reasons why survivors drift into such relationships are:

- They don't feel worthy of anything better.
- They stay isolated on the outer edges socially and do not reach out to others.
- They have a need to feel needed and therefore important to someone.

As the survivor grows in a healthy sense of self-worth, the attraction to more wholesome relationships becomes stronger, and the old relationships with users becomes less desirable. The change will tend to happen naturally. Some help will come from making the effort to reach out to others and interact with them. Some will come from steering the very needy people into professional counseling. Some help will come from becoming less available to the takers without feeling guilty. There is a time and place to help others, but no one can afford to let someone else take over his or her whole life. Not even a professional counselor can afford to do that. We must all have boundaries for our time, efforts, and relationships. We all need some private time for ourselves as well as healthy interaction with others.

> Joe had a problem with another male who always needed to be around him, always wanted to be available to help in any way. Joe could not go anywhere without this person showing up and attaching himself. Joe tried to avoid him, but it didn't work. The guy just kept showing up. Joe couldn't get two steps out of the church aisle to speak to a friend without being cornered by this guy.
>
> Enough was enough. Joe finally explained the problem to the man. Joe had other friends he needed to speak to, but he was always prevented from doing so. The man was a bit hurt, but he did change his behavior.

Summary

Make no mistake about it. Every step taken up to this point will be incomplete unless there is an earnest desire to grow to maturity. As necessary as it is, sharing inner pain, anger, and hurt will not in and of itself bring about healing. *The ultimate goal of healing is that of change from the helpless and hurting victim to a mature person who is able, with the help of God, to face with honesty, courage, and faith whatever life may bring.* Learn to face the problems of life head on and take whatever constructive action is needed to bring about resolution with sensitivity and caring toward everyone concerned. Such is the demonstration of true healing that has taken place within.

A number who have read through these pages will recognize their own deep turmoil. If that is the case, seek out a professional counselor or therapist to help you find healing. See appendix B for some basic guidelines for finding a good therapist who can assure that your journey will be a successful one.

The final destination is that of health, normalcy, and the ability to develop one's potential in life. The steps to full and complete healing for each survivor include the following:

1. *Find the roots of the problem.* Don't be satisfied with superficial solutions to complex problems. Dig out the truth of what really did happen in the past that still impacts your life in the present.
2. *Get at the long buried feelings; look for constructive ways to release them.* Each one that is released in a proper way adds to your present freedom and inner strength.
3. *Discover the wrong beliefs about yourself.* Challenge them. Straighten out tangled thinking. Develop an accurate view of yourself as a person and of others around you. Put these new beliefs to work in your life.
4. *Seek positive, supportive, and confidential friendships.* This will help you understand how others value you and to experience genuine caring without strings attached.
5. *Seek out balanced information on the healthy expression of sexuality.* Learn what are proper boundaries and work hard at establishing those. Learn what is normal sexuality and seek to apply it to your life.
6. *Approach confrontation cautiously.* Recognize that confrontation of one's abuser can have a very posi-

tive effect. It can also backfire rather badly if you are
not well prepared or do not go at it properly.

7. *Do forgive your abuser for wrongs done and yourself
   for being vulnerable* once you are far enough along in
   your healing to do so. This step can bring even greater
   freedom.

8. *Take charge of your life.* Learn to face life squarely,
   handle the challenges that come to you, and move on.
   Learn to look at your abuse as something that happened, but something you survived and which no
   longer is a major focus of your life. Move on to other
   challenges.

*The good news is that the survivor can find a normal life,
and he or she can develop God-given talents into a useful
and productive life. A life of fulfillment can be found!* Some
scars of the journey may remain, but the old problems no
longer take control. The survivor can now make healthy
choices with healthy results. The mind is clear; the fog is
gone. The inner self is at peace. The burden is so much
lighter. Not all problems have disappeared, but compared
to what it was, life seems so unbelievably good. The journey
was well worth it. The struggle has not been in vain. The
survivor has found a welcome home from the long and arduous journey.

Part 5
Protection for the Future

12

Protecting One's Own Family

But if anyone causes one of these little ones who believe in me to sin, it would be better for him to have a large mill-stone hung around his neck and to be drowned in the depths of the sea.

Matthew 18:6

How can anyone protect one's own family from the horrors of childhood sexual abuse? How can a survivor who has struggled through the tangle of such trauma prevent history from repeating itself? Survivors who have worked hard to make a decent life are worried about the safety of their children. Their greatest nightmare is that their children might disappear or be tortured and abused at the hands of strangers. Such dangers are not to be taken lightly, for we are daily bombarded by media reports that show that children indeed can be at risk.

The statistics indicate, however, that by far the majority of abuse comes from people who are already a part of the family, close relatives, or at least are well known and trusted within the family circle. Although most survivors of abuse do *not* themselves become abusers, statistics do indicate that most abusers of children have already been through abuse in their own childhood. They abuse other children as they themselves have been abused.

Another part of the equation lies in the repetitive patterns found in dysfunctional families. People tend to marry into or follow familiar patterns. For example, those who have grown up in alcoholic homes tend to either become alcoholics or marry one. After many years of struggle, the sober spouse may leave that dysfunctional system, determined to get out of that mess. What really seems strange is that many of them unknowingly then marry another alcoholic. Somehow they missed the signs.

The same patterns show up with survivors of sexual abuse. They tend to have similar patterns repeated in their own families. Survivors of sexual abuse in childhood may then marry someone who becomes abusive to their own children. Some survivors have children who are abused by someone outside the home. A few become abusive themselves. The repeating cycle of abuse may then go on for generations if left unchecked.

What can be done to break the chain of abuse? Can we make a difference? Indeed we can. Let us look at a few strategies.

Know What Is Happening with Your Kids

Each survivor needs to take charge of his or her own family. The task of parenting is basically a twenty-year project, starting from total control of the child at infancy, to zero control at adulthood.[1] Throughout that growing-up period, the parents have a responsibility to protect and educate their children about dangers they may not be well prepared to handle themselves. Parents do not need to be paranoid about every possible thing that could go wrong, but they do need to be alert as to what is happening to their own children. The principles to follow are vital:

1. *Know where your children are.* Insist on your kids telling you where they are and who they are with. This is not a luxury. This is your right as a parent who is responsible for their welfare. You need to know where to find your kids and what they are do-

ing. The idea of *accountability*, not to mention the possibility that you could show up unexpectedly, acts as a deterrent. It also communicates that we are all accountable to someone in life. Large periods of time unsupervised leave too much room for too many wrong things to happen. Do not hound them every minute, but keep your eyes and ears open. If there is an unusual amount of silence or hedging about what is happening, that's the time to look into matters.[2]

The lack of accountability to parents can give children the message that the parent does not care that much what happens. Kids are thus tempted to do things together they might not otherwise do. Too much time without supervision can make it more difficult for the child to resist the manipulations of another toward something sexual or inappropriate.

2. *Know who your child's friends are and what they are like.* Do not allow your child to run with just anyone. If your child tends to disappear into the woods or some place with an older kid or adult, ask questions about exactly what they do there. You may want to ask more direct questions about sexual activities. You may not get a direct answer, but your knowledge of your own child and his or her reaction will give you needed clues. As a parent you do have a right to curtail such visits if you have good reason to suspect something is wrong. Your child may be upset at your restrictions, but he or she will thank you in the end. *A child finds it very difficult to refuse an older kid and depends on the parent for needed protection.* Be sure to keep your end of the responsibility.[3]

3. *Keep an open communication with your children.* This is vital. A child who is used to talking openly with his or her parents will be much more likely to either volunteer a problem or to answer direct ques-

tions when asked. A sudden change from openness with accompanying uncharacteristic behavior should set off alarm bells and cause you to investigate what might be happening. Open communication with your children makes them less vulnerable to abuse in the first place. A child who feels loved and cared about is less vulnerable and more able to resist a potential abuser. Therefore, make time in your busy schedule to be friends with your children. Take time to play with them; do things they like to do. Be available to listen. Be slow to condemn and quick to understand. Show your caring in every possible way.[4]

4. *Know the person with whom you leave your children.* Sometimes you will need to leave your kids with someone. Do all the checking you can reasonably do about baby-sitters, friends, or even relatives. Try to get your children to tell you different things they did with the person who cared for them. Be tuned-in to changes in voice, posture, or body language that might indicate a problem. If your child seems really upset about staying with a certain person, try to make other arrangements. Something may be happening there of a damaging nature. If possible, find out from your child the source of unpleasantness he or she wants to avoid. Remember that most childhood sexual abuse is not done by strangers but usually by someone well known and respected by the family. Again, you don't have to be paranoid or overprotective, but do be alert.

Inform Your Kids

Tell your kids what is appropriate behavior and what is not. Start to teach them at an early age basics about their bodies. Let them know what to do when someone has gone beyond what is normal and healthy. For example:

1. Make it very clear at early ages that *nobody* has a right to touch them in private places.
2. Tell them that if someone tries to touch them inappropriately, they are to yell, kick, scream, fight, whatever is necessary to let the other person know they want no part of this under any circumstances. The child's resistance in itself may be sufficient to scare away a potential offender who is afraid of being found out.
3. Tell your child that if anyone, including relatives, does try to molest him or her by touching in private places, the child is to tell you immediately, no matter what threats the other person may make. The same goes for pornographic material or X-rated movies. Make sure the child understands that he or she will not be blamed for someone else's wrong actions but will be rewarded for telling the truth. Tell the child not to be afraid of whatever threats the person makes, even if the person threatens to harm the parents. Tell him or her that it is your job to protect your children, and that you can take care of yourself, even if you need to call the police.

Be sure to give your children specific instructions of what to do in the kinds of situations they might meet. Some years ago, one of our daughters was walking home from kindergarten, about a half mile away. A car stopped beside her, and a stranger offered her candy and promised to take her home. Since she had been instructed beforehand what to do, she refused and ran to her mother. She was able to describe the car well enough so that the police found the person and took him into custody. Previous instruction paid off and prevented a potential disaster.

However, since most abuse takes place with people whom our children already know, not strangers, it is doubly important that we explain carefully just what they must do when someone wants to touch them in wrong places or get them interested in pictures of nudity or sexual activity.

Probably the greatest gift you can give your children that will in turn help protect them from being molested is a solid home where love and caring is modeled and where healthy parenting is practiced. Kids need *a good balance of love and discipline.* Once they have that, they are able to stand against a lot of things. They not only need to be told they are loved, but they need to see and experience it on a daily basis. Kids who feel secure in their parents' love and who have a good sense of right and wrong will be less susceptible to the persuasions of manipulative and evil people.

The child from a dysfunctional home is much more vulnerable to abuse than one from a healthy home. Homes where there is alcoholism, frequent conflict, verbal arguing, screaming and shouting, or physical combat are much more at risk. Parental neglect—where parents are absent a lot or too occupied with their own pursuits to be involved with their children—likewise produces kids at risk.

Children growing up in such homes are missing some basics in their emotional development. Most of them are very lonely, feel neglected and unloved, and are starving for affection. They do not feel important to anyone. They feel and act differently socially. Instead of being in the middle of games with friends, they are often hanging back, on the outer edges of the social interaction, or sometimes completely alone away from the others. They are often quiet, unhappy, and have little to say.

Child abusers pick up on the message of a hurt and lonely child very quickly and soon move in as predators after a wounded prey. Child molesters do not bother much with kids who are well adjusted. They look for emotionally needy kids simply because they sense they can have more success with their perverted plans. They zero in on the loneliness and offer friendship and caring by simply giving the child some much-needed attention. Once they have gained enough ground with the vulnerable child, they move on to more sexually oriented pursuits. Thus they capture the wounded child to use for their own selfish pursuits. The quiet, lonely children need our protection and our attention, not our criticism.

Things to Look For

"If my child is afraid to tell me, how will I know if he or she has been molested by someone? What clues would I look for? I can't be questioning my child all the time about everything and everybody." The following lists are not complete, but they give some important clues to tip you off to foul play.

Physical Indicators

> pain or itching in genital areas
> bruises or bleeding in external genital, vaginal, or anal areas
> torn, stained, or bloody underclothing
> difficulty walking or sitting
> venereal disease, especially before teen years

Behavioral Indicators

> unwilling to change for gym or participate in physical education
> withdrawal, fantasy, or infantile behavior
> bizarre, sophisticated, or unusual sexual knowledge or behavior
> poor peer relationships
> delinquent or runaway behavior
> reports of sexual assault by a caretaker

Emotional Indicators

> *Infant and Toddler:*
> irritability
> feeding difficulties

sleep disturbances
change in level of activity

School-Age Child:
behavioral problems; changes from past behavior patterns
anxieties not previously observed
sleep disturbances
frightful dreams, e.g., being kidnapped, attacked, taken
   away, hunted down, shot at, etc.
withdrawn attitude; uncomfortable around people

Adolescent:
fright and confusion
guilt feelings
anger, acting out behavior
depressive affect

No one of these symptoms is of itself necessarily a reason to conclude that your child has been molested, except for the more obvious physical indicators. But if some of these fit your child, especially if you have observed an abrupt change in behavior or demeanor, by all means start asking questions in an effort to find the cause.

How to Help Keep Young People Safe

Recently I came across a listing of helpful suggestions that I would like to pass on to you.

Things to Do as a Family

1. An unattended child is a child at risk. Arrange with your child an alternative well-lit place, and preferably with someone, where he or she can wait if you are delayed.
2. Whenever possible, have children walk in pairs or groups. Children should always travel the same way home. No shortcuts through isolated areas.

3. Know the adults who work with your children both at school and in recreational programs.

4. Use a secret family code or password. Children should never go with anyone, not even close family friends, unless such friends are able to give the child the password. After the password has been used in a given situation, a new one should be selected.

5. Don't allow your children to go to a public washroom unattended.

6. Check your baby-sitter's credentials thoroughly. Review the latchkey rules if your child has to be at home alone after school. He or she should be taught never to admit visitors and never to let telephone callers know he or she is alone. If you don't have an answering machine, instruct your child to say that you can't come to the phone right then, but that the caller should leave his or her name and number and you will call back.

Things to Tell Your Child

1. Explain to your children the difference between "good touches" and "bad touches" and encourage them to listen to their feelings. If their feelings say something is not right, they should refuse to be involved.

2. Give your children the self-confidence to assert themselves and refuse someone who wants to touch them or ask them to do something they feel is not right.

3. Give them permission to loudly say "No, don't touch me," and reassure your kids that it is not rude to do so.

What to Do if Your Child Tells You He or She Has Been Approached or Assaulted

1. If anyone, even someone they love, threatens to or does touch them in a way that doesn't feel right, impress on your children that they must come and tell

you. Explain that if an adult wants your child to have a secret that only the two can share, that is not right. Remind the child that you are the one responsible for the child's protection, and therefore you must be told about any intrusion by anyone.

2. Listen to your child and let him or her tell you in his or her own words or with drawings or dolls if that is easier. Don't inject *your* words or modify what is being said; your injected ideas might confuse the truth. Simply encourage the child to get it out. Ask questions to clarify your own understanding of what the child is saying. *Do* remain calm.

3. Younger children seldom lie about sexual abuse. Reassure the child that you believe what he or she has said and that you are glad to have been told about it.

4. Do not blame the child, show horror or anger, or encourage any belief in the child that this was his or her fault.

5. Support the child and recognize the child's feelings— whether they are anger, fear, sadness, or anxiety— and assure the child that you will protect him or her from any further abuse.

6. Let your child know that you are going to take steps to make this abuse stop. Don't burden the child with details about what happens next, but do give simple and direct answers to the child's questions, and explain why that action might be necessary. Explain that further action is required not only to stop the abuse to your own child, but for the protection of other children as well. Professionals can help you guide your child through this process.

7. If you suspect that your child or another has been abused, you *must* by law call the police or the child protection officials at once. In most states you can, if necessary, remain anonymous when calling on behalf of a child.

8. If your child is to be interviewed by a social worker or police officer, ensure that someone dear to the child is also present for support.[5]

Break the Cycle

No survivors who have been through the ravages of sexual abuse will want their children to suffer the same prolonged agony that has been theirs. I am sure that each parent will want to take every precaution possible to prevent that kind of tragedy from happening in whatever way possible. All of the suggestions given up to this point can be helpful, and I sincerely hope you as a parent will want to put every one of them into practice.

If you have been through a lot of trauma in your own childhood, I think that the greatest thing you can do for your kids is to give them the *gift of a parent who has found healing for himself or herself.* You will find it very hard to love your children adequately when your own experience of love has been twisted and betrayed. You will find it hard to correct and discipline your children appropriately when you carry a deep, underlying well of anger that can easily be triggered by the normal frustrations of raising kids. You will find it difficult to instill a good sense of self-esteem within your child if you hate yourself. You will find it difficult to train a child to find a good balance of responsibility and freedom if you yourself are weighed down with guilt and shame. You may find it difficult to do fun things with your children simply because you are not sure how to have fun yourself and are too focused on your own problems. If you have difficulty in relationships with the opposite sex, your child may well have similar difficulty. If your marriage is in bad shape because of carryovers from your past, your child may well have future difficulty in marriage also. Negative attitudes about sexuality are very easily transmitted without words. With so much sexual emphasis in our society, every child needs a healthy sense of his or her own self and sexuality to survive.

The most important person in your child's life is *you*. If you are still struggling with the aftereffects of trauma from your own childhood, by all means, *get the help you need so that you in turn can raise healthy children.*

Summary

A survivor can break the repeating cycle of sexual abuse by giving careful attention to the welfare of one's own children as well as focusing on one's own personal healing. Ordinary protection includes such things as knowing where your children are, who they are with, and carefully checking anyone who temporarily takes care of your kids. An atmosphere of open and honest sharing and frequent messages of love and caring help immeasurably. Give your kids permission to do the unusual, to kick, scream, and be rude if someone tries to touch them in private places. Have a no-secrets rule, and be sure to reward for truth. Look out for physical indicators or behavioral and emotional change. Give specific instruction on things your kids need to know to get out of difficult situations. Do role-playing to train them in proper responses. Give your children a safe, friendly, loving home where they are free to share and talk about anything.

By putting all of these strategies to work, we can break the cycle of abuse and keep it from being repeated from one generation to the next within our family line.

13

About Abusers

Have mercy on me, O God,
according to your unfailing love;
according to your great compassion
blot out my transgressions.
Wash away all my iniquity
and cleanse me from my sin.
For I know my transgressions,
and my sin is always before me.
Against you, you only, have I sinned
and done what is evil in your sight,
so that you are proved right when you speak
and justified when you judge.
Surely I was sinful at birth,
sinful from the time my mother conceived me.
Surely you desire truth in the inner parts;
you teach me wisdom in the inmost place.

Create in me a pure heart, O God,
and renew a steadfast spirit within me.
Do not cast me from your presence
or take your Holy Spirit from me.
Restore to me the joy of your salvation
and grant me a willing spirit, to sustain me.
Then I will teach transgressors your ways,
and sinners will turn back to you.

Psalm 51:1–6, 10–13

(A psalm of David when the prophet Nathan
came to him after David had committed
adultery with Bathsheba.)

"I don't want to know about abusers. I think they are the scum of the earth. I hate them. I don't know how you can even write about them, and I certainly don't want to read it. They don't deserve the time of day as far as I am concerned. They should all be locked up and the key thrown away!"

A lot of survivors of childhood sexual abuse will feel this way, and for good reason. There is no denying the tremendous destruction sexual abusers have brought to the lives of their victims. If you are one of those who can't stand the thought of a child abuser, you certainly have my permission to skip this chapter. It's not for you. I don't find it easy to write about abusers either. They are a pitiful bunch who lead very troubled lives and have sought to solve their problems and needs by exploiting others.

Remember, though, if we are going to stop the repeating cycle of childhood sexual abuse, then we had better give some serious thought to how to help abusers so that they don't repeat these acts again. The average offender without intervention may abuse as many as one hundred children during his or her lifetime.[1] Anything that we can do to stop that horrendous pattern will be of great service to children and families everywhere.

Since most therapeutic work with perpetrators of childhood sexual abuse is done in institutional settings, not many therapists in private practice have extensive contact with them. A lot is still not well known in working with offenders, but there is some good material available that can help us understand the needs of these very troubled people. Therapeutic intervention with abusers is generally considered a specialty, so most of what is written here will be based on the writings of others who have firsthand experience in the field.

Characteristics of Abusers

Abusers of children don't look any different than anyone else. They can be members of the immediate family, extended family, caretakers, respected friends, or community leaders. They don't have the appearance of sleaze as we might imagine. They can come from all educational or occupational backgrounds. Their race, religion, intelligence, mental status, or socioeconomic class has little to do with the problem. Nor are Christians exempt from this type of behavior, for they contain the same proportionate number of abusers as the general population. Some of the more serious offenders are professing Christians.

According to Grant L. Martin, Ph.D., a typical religious offender is likely to have a rigid, highly structured religious lifestyle. He or she will be very conscientious, moralistic, yet frustrated and strongly opinionated, with an outspoken view of right and wrong, regardless of his or her private behavior. The offender is usually a good provider and active church attender but has a poor self-concept, lacks full control of his or her impulses, is socially isolated, feels needy and neglected, lacks intimacy in his or her life, has a less than satisfactory marriage, and was abused or emotionally neglected as a child. The religious offender will not generally go outside the family for sexual satisfaction. He or she does not usually view his or her own incestuous behavior as immoral or unacceptable because it occurs within the family. The abuser finds that adult relationships require negotiation, mutuality, reciprocity, and shared commitment, and such relationships are either unavailable or overtaxing. The abuser, therefore, turns to his or her child for sexual gratification of emotional needs without the demands of adult responsibility.[2]

To understand abusers, we must know what they are like. Some general characteristics include:

- Sex offenders seldom are truthful about their behavior. They will minimize, deny, and lie about what happened. If they say the abuse happened once or twice, you can be sure it happened many times.
- Sex offenders seldom express remorse or any sense of wrongdoing. They do not see their actions as evil, nor

do they seem to be aware of the feelings of their victim. Their focus is self-gratification and power.

- Sex offenders are most concerned with the consequences of being caught. They can, therefore, be very manipulative and will try to mobilize the support of respected persons as character witnesses on their behalf.
- Sex offenders are usually repeat offenders and will continue to abuse others until they are stopped. Professional counseling by itself does not seem to help that much. Nor does their conscience seem to be adequate. The one thing that does seem to work the best is the legal system. Jail, or the threat of it, along with required counseling as long as possible has seemed to be the most effective treatment thus far.
- Most sex offenders are looking for a quick fix. The idea of long-term therapy is not on their agenda.
- The typical sex offender has multiple layers of denial and deceit and a number of personality qualities of a sociopath.[3] The denial and deceit must be addressed straightforwardly before any change can be hoped for.[4]
- Sex offenders see themselves as helpless victims of outside forces. They do not feel much sense of personal power over their life. In fact, they feel quite powerless and insignificant.
- Sex offenders have a continual feeling of isolation from others and feel very alone. They lack any consistent sense of intimate attachment or relatedness. They are close to nobody.
- Sex offenders have an underlying mood of emptiness, fearfulness, and depression. This combines with low self-esteem and poor self-confidence to make them oversensitive to perceived criticisms, put-downs, exploitations, and rejections from a hostile world.
- Sex offenders' lack of security and comfort, along with their deficient empathic skills, lead them to avoid

adult relationships. They substitute fantasy for reality and replace adults with children who complement their own immaturity.

- Sex offenders become emotionally overinvested in their victim. Abusers try to monopolize the victim's time and restrict his or her outside interests and activities. Abusers regard their victim as more of a peer than a child. They feel a narcissistic (self-loving) sense of ownership or entitlement to the victim and project their own needs and desires on the child. Abusers become preoccupied with sexual fantasies about the victim and develop a sense of pleasure, comfort, and power in the relationship.[5]

Many of the features of the sexual offender are found in the addictive personality as well. These features include such things as:

- The sex offender has a tendency to move from crisis to crisis, never becoming settled in a satisfying day-to-day existence. The feeling of mastery over his or her environment is lacking.
- The sex offender is a dependent personality who cannot stand alone without continuous external support. He or she has real difficulty handling problems alone.
- The sex offender has an impulsive nature and inability to defer gratification, yet he or she gets little long-term pleasure in life.
- The sex offender has low self-esteem, a core sense of worthlessness with an extreme vulnerability to criticism, and a tendency to be motivated by shame and guilt. Often he or she may become obsessed with self-criticism while minimizing his or her strengths.
- The sex offender has a history of untreated psychosocial trauma in his or her childhood, which has left him or

her emotionally immature, fearful, and unable to trust others. Often he or she was a victim of child abuse.

- The sex offender needs the comfort of well-established and well-defined routines to provide the necessary reassurance to go about daily living. He or she goes to great lengths to maintain strict routines and rituals.[6]

Types of Offenders

Writers in the field of treatment of sexual offenders of children make frequent reference to the work of A. Nicholas Groth. He classifies sexual offenses into two main categories: *rape* and *molestation.*

Rape of a child is usually an expression of rage, power needs, and sadistic pleasure, and accounts for 15 to 20 percent of child abuse. These abusers will use threats, intimidation, or physical force. They may tell the child victim that they will beat or even kill him or her or throw the child out on the street if the child does not comply.

Molestation, on the other hand, is more of a seductive act in which the molester seeks mutual enjoyment, acceptance, and affection. These account for 80 to 85 percent of child abuse. Molesters usually take time to set up the victim, usually an emotionally hungry and compliant child, with a progression of behavior beginning with nongenital acts. They may promise to buy something nice in return or treat this as a special game that will be "our secret."

Of these two types of abusers, the rapist and the molester, Dr. Groth differentiates between two types of development of the offender's social and sexual orientation: the fixated and the regressed. The difference has a lot to do with treatment options.

Fixated offenders are those whose sociosexual development was arrested or stopped during childhood, adolescence, or early adult years. The sexual orientation of fixated offenders is focused on children. They are sexually drawn to children in that they identify with the child and appear in some ways to want to remain children themselves. They tend to adapt their behavior and interest to the level of the child in an effort to have the child accept them as an equal.[7] In other words, they have remained a child who never grew past a certain point in life.

Regressed offenders on the other hand, are reacting to conflicts and problems in adult relationships. These offenders fail to cope with life's stressors and impulsively offend against children when crises arise in their lives. They are primarily oriented toward adults, the majority of them being married. When they offend, they suspend their usual value system or rationalize that what they are doing is allowable. They are distressed by their own abusive behavior and do experience guilt, shame, and remorse after an incident, much like an alcoholic or other addictive personalities. They may be drawn to children in an attempt to replace their adult relationships, which have become unfulfilling or full of conflict. These offenders thus select a child as a substitute.[8]

The following chart (see page 226) may be helpful in understanding the information from A. Groth. It shows a comparison of the regressed and the fixated offender.[9]

David Finkelhor, Ph.D., and Linda Meyer Williams, Ph.D., who are sociologists at the Family Research Laboratory of the University of New Hampshire, recently completed the most thorough study to date of men who have sexually abused their daughters. They set out to find the various possible causes of incest by these fathers and have shed some new light on the subject. The most significant finding is that there are many paths to incestuous behavior, and there is not just one type of man who commits such abuse. The types of offenders fall into five categories:

1. Twenty-six percent were *sexually preoccupied*. Each man in this category had a clear and conscious (often

Offender Comparison Chart

Regressed Offender	Fixated Offender
1. Primary sexual orientation— normally relates to age-mates	1. Primary sexual orientation— normally relates to a child
2. Pedophilic interests— emerges in adulthood	2. Pedophilic interests— emerges in adolescence
3. A precipitating stressor is evident or identifiable	3. No precipitating stressor
4. Sexually abusive acts are episodic, usually under stress	4. Persistent sexually abusive acts of a chronic and compulsive nature
5. The initial sexual act may be on the impulse, followed by shock and dismay	5. The sexual offense is preplanned from beginning to end
6. Misperceives the child as a peer	6. Identifies with the child. Misperceives self as a child
7. Primary targets are opposite-sex victims	7. Primary targets are same-sex victims
8. Child sexual contact is concurrent with age-mates	8. Child sexual contact primarily, little with age-mates
9. Focus is on the offender's own sexual arousal	9. Focus is on sexual arousal of the child, an act of power
10. Offense is more likely alcohol related	10. Usually no alcohol or drug use
11. Traditional lifestyle but poorly developed peer relationships	11. Exhibits chronic immaturity, arrested development
12. Abuses as a response to overwhelming life stress	12. Abuses in response to developmental issues, as a child

obsessive) sexual interest in his daughter. It was often the case that he regarded his daughter as a sex object almost from birth. The thinking of these men was so sexualized that they simply projected their sexual need onto everybody and everything. The child may have been the one who was most easily manipulated to satisfy the preoccupation. Many of these offenders had been sexually abused as children.

2. About one-third, 33 percent, were *adolescent regressive*. Each of these men became sexually interested in

his daughter when she entered puberty. They said they were "transfixed" by her body's changes. These men acted and sounded like young adolescents themselves when they talked about their daughters. "The father-adult in me had shut down," said one offender, "and I was like a kid again."

3. About 20 percent of the sample were *instrumental self-gratifiers*. When a man in this group abused his daughter, he thought of someone else—his wife, or his daughter as an adult. He used his daughter's body as a receptacle and blocked from his mind what he was doing. The daughter was a nonperson at that point. This abuse was more sporadic. The men did worry about the harm they were causing and felt great guilt. To alleviate the guilt, some convinced themselves that the daughter was aroused.

4. Just over 10 percent were *emotionally dependent*: needy, lonely, depressed. They thought of themselves as failures and looked to the daughter for "close, exclusive, emotionally dependent relationships," including sexual gratification, which they linked to intimacy and not particularly to their sexual qualities. The relationship had more of a romantic flavor. A man in this group would describe his daughter as he might describe an adult lover.

5. About 10 percent were *angry retaliators*. These fathers were the most likely to have criminal histories of assault and rape. This type abused a daughter out of anger at her or, more often, at her mother for neglecting or deserting him. Some denied any sexual feelings for the daughter. It was a way to get back at the wife for making the daughter the center of her life and leaving him out. Some were aroused by the violence of their acts of abuse.

Other findings from the study included:

1. Thirty-three percent of these men reported being under the influence of alcohol when the abuse occurred, and 10 percent reported using drugs. The substance abuse may have been used to lower their inhibitions to abuse.
2. Forty-three percent of the men felt that their marriage relationship was part of the reason for the incest, but the wife was rarely the only factor involved.
3. Significantly, 70 percent of the men said they themselves had been sexually abused in childhood. Half were physically abused by the father, and almost half, 44 percent, had been physically abused by the mother. While certainly not all who are abused go on to become perpetrators, it is critical to learn more about how child sexual victimization affects male sexual development and male sexual socialization.[10]

Women Sexual Offenders

What can we learn about females who have sexually abused children under their care? What patterns can we see with them? Psychologist Ruth Mathews of St. Paul, Minnesota, conducted a study of one hundred female sex offenders—sixty-five adult women and thirty-five adolescent girls. She found they fell into four major categories:

1. *Teacher-Lover.* These are usually made up of older women who have sex with a young adolescent. This type often goes unnoticed because the behavior is socially sanctioned.
2. *Experimenter-Exploiter.* These are usually girls who come from rigid families where sex education is condemned or forbidden. They may use baby-sitting as an opportunity to explore small children. Many of these offenders don't know what they are doing, have never heard of or experienced masturbation, and are

terrified of sex. Their curiosity becomes aroused, then trouble may follow.

3. *Predisposed.* These women are predisposed to offend because of their own history of severe physical and/or sexual abuse. The victims are often their own children or siblings. The abuser may have been treated very badly as a child, and feeling more like an animal, thus doesn't realize her own children are human beings.

4. *Male-Coerced Women.* These are women who abuse children because men force them to. These women have a history of sexual abuse in their background, though probably not as severe as the predisposed offender. As teens they were isolated loners but anxious to belong. Many are married to sex offenders who may abuse the children for a long time without the wife's knowledge. Eventually she is brought into it and forced to involve her own children in abuse.[11]

Many of the female abusers were themselves abused from about age two onward by many family members. They received very little nurturing, and most of what they received was by their abuser. Thus they came to link abuse with caring. Such female abusers, like male abusers, will molest many children throughout their lifetime. They do, however, seem to have more remorse for their actions than their male counterparts.[12]

Abuse by female abusers, however, is underreported. No one really knows the extent of the problem. Just as for many years it was thought the only victims were female and their abusers were male, time has brought to light that large numbers of males were abused as children as well. While the majority of these seemed to be abused by males, an increasing number of male victims are revealing abuse by females. Just as male victims tend not to consider their experience as child abuse, there is an even greater reluctance to define male childhood sexual abuse by an older female as abnormal. Clinical experience indicates that the damage is just as great, the long-range effects on the male victim just as detrimental, and the need for therapeutic intervention just as vital.

Children Who Molest Children

We must be willing to accept the fact that not all abusers of children are adults. The evidence indicates that brother-sister sexual relationships may be *five times* as common as father-daughter incest. Yet sibling abuse has tended to be ignored, because the sibling abuse of one child toward another has generally been excused as "normal" behavior.[13]

What is the difference between normal curiosity between children and a sexual offense? Curiosity between boys and girls at roughly age five is quite normal. They each want to know what makes them different. But that's about as far as it goes. Explicit sexual information at such a young age is most likely to have been gained because they have observed specific sexual activities or have experienced it firsthand. With the availability of cable television that includes "adult" films or pornography, kids can learn a lot on their own before they should.

Sometimes preteens find out about masturbation quite accidentally, and they may be involved in some limited sexual touching of each other. Generally speaking, however, further specific interest in explicit sexual details does not naturally bloom until around puberty as hormones start to kick in and natural urges begin to make themselves known.

Adolescents will demonstrate a lot more interest in sexual things. Their hormones are beginning to become active; new urges and interests in the opposite sex begin to happen naturally. Kids talk a lot about it, and a lot of material is available to them. However, young kids who have a lot of knowledge and interest in oral, anal, and vaginal sex before adolescence have been unduly exposed somewhere.

The ingredients of abuse differ from ordinary child curiosity in that molestation includes trickery, clever persuasion, or force. Though young and inexperienced, the child seems to know that this is wrong and feels guilty and shameful. The betrayal of trust and confusion caused by the sense of excitement that has been stirred long before the child is ready adds to the problem, and long-lasting damage results.

Eliana Gil, Ph.D., indicates that, though still sparse, an increasing amount of information is coming to the forefront about children who molest other children. Their ages vary from young children to adolescents. Some are as young as two and a half years old. That's hard to comprehend! Such behavior for very young children is a symptom of some sort of underlying problem. Help is needed.[14]

There are generally four categories of child victims who are molested by other children:

1. *Siblings and other family members.* Young sex offenders may choose to molest a younger sibling or relative. These may be blood relatives such as cousins, nephews, or nieces, or they may be relationships or familiar roles such as adopted, stepfamilies, live-ins, etc.

2. *Wards.* Wards are children who are being cared for by an older child, such as a baby-sitter. The child is left under the authority of the baby-sitter and told to obey. The molester may begin with play and become progressively more sexual and compelling. Such situations could go on undetected for long periods of time, since most child victims do not volunteer information about their molestation.

3. *Acquaintances.* Some molested children are not family but are known to the young offenders. These may be children in the neighborhood or school who share activities together. The young child may look up to

the older child, and thus feel flattered by the attention, while giving the older child a sense of power to be able to manipulate the younger child into experimentation with sexual activity.

4. *Strangers*. The least frequent type of offender is the one who looks for child victims wherever children frequent. "Stalking" behavior on the part of a child indicates a very real need for professional help.[15]

Gil goes on to explain that the basic characteristics of children who molest are becoming clearer. Close parallels to adults who molest are quite apparent.

- *Denial*. Denial characterizes all sex offenders, young and old. They usually deny that they have done any such thing. They don't want to be found out. Since their behavior was purposely secretive, being caught can cause great pain, fear, shame, and embarrassment. To protect themselves, most insist they are not guilty and express outrage that anyone would accuse them of such a thing, even when confronted with clear and undeniable evidence.

- *Immaturity*. Most children who molest are immature. They are unable to think through what they are doing. They want things right now and cannot tolerate being frustrated. They act without thinking about consequences. They have to be taught to think before they act and to delay some of the things they want to a more appropriate time and place.

- *Low self-esteem*. Children who molest other children do not feel good about themselves and generally put others down. Many sex offenders describe themselves as "bad, ugly, fat, dorky, nerd," or other negative adjectives that may be in vogue at the time. They may feel like social outcasts. Even those who on the surface seem to have positive descriptions of themselves are found to have problems of self-esteem or self-doubt within.

- *Sexual confusion and stimulation.* Many young sex offenders have had ready access to Playboy channels on TV or find a way to get the X-rated movies at the local video store or find pornographic magazines. Materials of this nature teach boys to be aggressive, be sexual, and "get what you want" at the expense of the other person. Such exposure without teaching of values, morals, and appropriateness leaves a young person lost on a sea of desire.

  Many young people do not have the inner resources to resist the powerful force of sexual stimulation. Many have relentless peer pressure to become sexually active and thus follow the suggestiveness of what they see and hear. These youngsters may then convince themselves that molesting a child is okay, doesn't hurt anyone, and certainly relieves the peer pressure to gain knowledge and experience. When the behavior is not stopped, the offending child may further think about his or her victim, get sexually excited, and have long fantasies about sexual activity. The young sex offender begins to associate sexual excitement and pleasure with younger children, which can then become a fixed pattern.

- *Learned behavior.* In many cases, the young offender learned to molest others because he or she was first molested. This youngster as a victim may have felt so confused, scared, or stimulated by what happened that the behavior is repeated in an effort to make sense of what happened. Though it is hard to understand why a child who has been hurt would want to cause another the same pain, there can be a compulsive need to repeat what is familiar, which brings less anxiety than learning a new way of behaving. The same dynamics are thus repeated over and over. There may also be the need to "master" earlier sexual experiences by creating a familiar scene, but this time the former victim is now in charge and in control of the outcome. Repeated abuse of others may be the only clue that an abuser gives of his or her own abuse.

Young male sex offenders in particular have a very hard time talking about being molested. They feel that they should have escaped, stopped it, or somehow been able to defend themselves. After all, that is what "men" are supposed to be able to do. Victims who have turned offenders need help both with victim and offender issues.[16] The problem will not usually go away by itself, and usually professional therapy is required.

Treatment of Abusers

Most abusers do not serve a prison sentence longer than ten years, and most are back out in the community within two or three years. What then? Has the prison term helped? Are children now safe? Probably not. An offender who comes out of prison without intensive and adequate treatment is very likely to begin the same pattern all over again, putting many more children at risk.

What kind of treatment program is called for, and what are its essential ingredients? In their book, *Treating Perpetrators of Sexual Abuse,* Ingersoll and Patton have outlined several steps, learned from their experience in the field, that they believe are essentials. Let me share these steps with you:

Assuming Responsibility

The first vital step in a recovery process is to get through the denial by getting the offender to assume responsibility for his crime. A tough and tender approach must be used. The therapist may appeal to the offender to assist in the healing of the child victim by appropriate placement of the guilt so that the child can be set free from his or her own inappropriate self-blame. The counselor may offer to help the offender through the disclosure process with the police and family. The counselor needs to reinforce respect for the offender for admitting to guilt. *The primary object of this step is for the offender to assume responsibility for the crime.*

Shame

Many abusers are either shriveled up with shame or well fortified against it by layer upon layer of false bravado. Sometimes they have fooled themselves into believing they are safe from feeling shame again.

Shame can have its origins in very early ages. If a child grows up in a home devoid of nurturing by loving parents, he or she begins to take on a message of shame. "I must have done something wrong, otherwise Daddy and Mommy would love me and take care of me." The conviction of an underlying flaw grows within the child. The child then looks to his or her environment for confirmation of that flaw. The child develops defenses to protect self against absorbing any more shame. These defenses in turn allow the child either to maintain outward distance from potentially shaming or blaming others, or to focus inward, becoming hypervigilant to monitor potentially shameful behavior before it occurs. The social distance thus produced reinforces the message that the child is guilty of something so terrible that no one wants to be close, only now it feels like shame.

The child is now convinced that he or she is a bad person and may behave by acting out as a bad person. The message is, "I am a bad person; I do bad things." When the community moves in to put a damper on some of the acting out behavior, then the message is further reinforced, "You tell me I am bad; I must be bad." The underlying belief about self becomes more deeply ingrained. The whole process did not start with the child; it started with the child's caretaker. Convincing the abuser that he or she is not all bad is a big undertaking, but it must be done.

Take the concept of shame another step down the line
and apply it to an adult abuser who was once an abused
child. The abused child now moves into becoming a shamed
adult who then acts out his or her "badness" against another child who the abuser, in a regressed state, may view
as a peer. The importance of these connections are not to
excuse the abuser—for there are no excuses. Understanding
the natural progression of how all this could come about
can help the abuser to understand the whole baffling mess
a little better. It may also help others to understand a little
better. *The self-concept must change for there to be accompanying behavioral change.*

Self-Esteem

People who value themselves are more likely to value
others. People with no self-esteem are not likely to see value
in others either. The cycle of belief about themselves as bad
people is translated to bad behavior. For some abusers, the
ultimate bad is to abuse their own children.

Most abusers are stuck emotionally. They have drawn inward for protection and may seek to meet their physical and
emotional needs within the relative safety of their own families. Part of the work of therapy is to help abusers engage in
relationship risks and risks of all kinds in order to test themselves in the world and to establish limits and priorities.
Abusers have learned abusive behavior from abusive models. The therapeutic challenge, then, is to point out the flaws
in their models and to assist in growth with healthy models.
The therapist may be the first healthy model the person has
ever known. Abusers need to be trained to begin to look for
personal growth and strength in every new experience and
to begin to change their orientation away from a protective
one. Since most abusers have been criticized and judged by
others, a lot of retraining needs to take place. Once they
know they are capable of such growth, a great step forward
has been accomplished in improving self-esteem.

Abusers need a lot of help in managing their own lives and learning to make decisions. They need help in determining values in life, what is right and wrong, what is a good way of doing things, and what ways work against them. As people make decisions for themselves based on what they value, take charge of their own lives, and set their own life courses, self-esteem increases. Abusers have never had this ability. They have always blamed themselves for their own helplessness. They believe they were forced to do what they did to the child. That attitude is not acceptable and must be confronted head-on. Abusers must be made to see that they always have choices and that *they* decide what to do, even if by deciding not to decide. They will need to be constantly reminded of where they are going with their lives and what the rewards of the journey will be. This task will not always be easy, but it is essential.

The abuser will need help in regaining lost connectedness. For the abuser in prison, family connections are severed, community connection is broken, relationships with primary loved ones are shattered, connection to the workplace is interrupted, and the abuser feels like an alien. Work must be done to begin making reconnection with others where that may be possible.

Validation of the abuser as a human being with some worth and value will not be easy, but the therapist must set the pace. *As abusers learn to value themselves and others, they will have less need to hurt themselves or others.*

Loss

Abusers have suffered many losses by their own doing. They have lost the respect of friends, the community's sympathy, a job or business relations, the emotional support of extended family, and the right to involvement with their primary family. Interaction with all of these people is lost as well. Abusers are, therefore, more likely to respond to a car-

ing therapist. Even a small loss can appear large to someone
with already low self-esteem.

A lot of grief work needs to take place to deal with these
losses. For regressed offenders, their crime of child sexual
abuse followed closely after a life stressor such as the death
of a parent, multiple deaths, death of the abuser's abuser,
work-related losses, lost relationships, or changes in balance of power within the family. Abusers must work
through their grief and learn new coping strategies to replace the former patterns. Other loss-related issues include:

> Was there a lost opportunity to straighten out some un-
> resolved problem?
> Is there a relationship to be reinstated?
> Is the chance to recapture the lost childhood gone forever?

No matter what happened in the past, or what each of these
losses meant, the abuser must learn to take responsibility for
whatever choices and responses he or she made. *The recov-
ering abuser will need help in making appropriate responses.*

Forgiveness

The concept of forgiveness may at first seem repulsive, as
most people are bent toward punishment of abusers rather
than treatment and forgiveness. But the fact remains that
forgiveness can be a *very powerful step* in the healing process imperative to the recovery of abusers. Abusers need to
learn to:

> forgive themselves as abusers
> forgive themselves as victims
> find forgiveness between the victim and the abuser
> find forgiveness from the family
> forgive the one who was the abuser in their own life

Let us be clear, however, that forgiveness of an abuser
is not a simple task. It is not absolution for the offending

party; it is not condoning the injury suffered; it is not for-getting the crime committed; it is not retaliation for the in-jury. Forgiveness is a *process* of working through highly charged emotional responses to pain and injury in order to be able to move on with life. Forgiveness is a *process* in which the abuser invests a lot of time and energy to re-move the accumulation of emotional baggage that has blocked personal growth. This process is made up of six vital steps.

1. *Denial.* First, there is the abuser's denial of abusing children, and, second, denial of his or her own abuse at the hand of another. As the abuser explores his or her own experience as a victim, the reality of the abuser's crime and how it hurt the victim can be more adequately addressed. Abusers often actually believe they did not hurt the child victim and, therefore, are imprisoned wrongfully. By carefully comparing his or her own experience and all the pain that went with it, the abuser can gradually be helped to face up to the pain he or she has caused.

2. *Self-Blame.* As with any other victims of childhood sexual abuse, those who have become abusers have difficulty blaming the loved one who abused them in the first place. Therefore, they blame themselves: "I was a bad kid." "I was a sexy kid." "I made him an-gry." "I somehow encouraged it." The victim turned abuser must come to see where the real blame lies and correct his or her own self-concept.

   The abuser also needs to see that he or she did not start out as a bad person and did not need to do bad things. The abuser then must face the full responsibil-ity for his or her own abusive behavior and remove the burden of blame from the victim. Help is found in reconstructing what happened, then peeling away the layers of emotional response, exploring each as it emerges, and getting the abuser to own the blame where appropriate.

The therapeutic work for abusers is twofold: to accept in full the blame for what he or she did, while placing the blame for his or her own victimization with his or her abuser. It is necessary to be tender when dealing with the abuser's own abuse but tough in establishing blame for the abuser's actions.

3. *Victim Stage.* A victim's style of handling his or her world may be evidenced by whiny, self-pity, "poor me" actions; self-indulgent, destructive behavior such as substance abuse or eating disorders; or meanness as demonstrated by overt or unexpressed anger, excessive criticism, sarcasm, general irritability, or short temper. Help in the victim stage is facilitated by identifying which style of relating to the world the victim uses and how the victim benefits from that style, as well as how greater benefits can be achieved by more constructive expression of emotions. *Working through the victim stage helps the abuser to transpose that victim experience to an understanding of how his or her own victim feels.* Eventually the way may clear for the abuser to become available for confrontation by his or her own victim and any other injured parties as another big step toward healing.

4. *Anger.* Victims of abuse need the opportunity to vent their anger. Once they understand that their own victimization was done *to* them and not *by* them, they are free to vent the anger that they feel. Previously, they had turned the anger on themselves. Now the anger must be expressed outwardly as the victim rages about what was done and becomes determined to never let this happen again. It is important to help him or her discover practical ways of venting anger that do not hurt others.

The abuser may then be able to help in the healing of his or her victim by being willing to be confronted in a healthy manner. However, if the abuser has not first worked through his or her own victimization, he or she will probably meet the victim's anger with defensiveness and denial, thus blocking the victim's healing. *Becoming able to handle the victim's anger is equally important to the healing of the abuser.*

5. *Survivor.* While the theme of a victim is "poor me," the theme of a survivor is, "It was awful, but I made it. Hurrah for me!" Survivors begin to trust themselves and their own intuitions. Survivors allow themselves a sense of humor. They become helpful to others. They develop trust of others and can relate to them positively.

Abusers must go through the same process. *Once abusers can see that they are not limited by their own victimization, they are free to grow in self-esteem and become optimistic about a future.* Abusers will need help in learning how to handle stressful situations, how to relate to family and community, and ways of becoming stronger physically, emotionally, interpersonally, and economically. At this point thought needs to be given about ways to make restitution to self, victim, family, and community.

6. *Integration.* As victims of sexual abuse integrate the abuse into their overall life, they are no longer focused on their abuse as the one major event in their lives. They see their own victimization as only one event in the total picture of their lives. At this point, the former victim is able to let go of the emotional impact of the victimization and replace it with a sense of peace. The therapeutic work at this stage centers around a redefinition of self, assessing strengths and abilities, setting new goals, and reevaluating the experience of being victimized.

Abusers need to reach this same stage of integration just as much as victims. They have to reach beyond both victim and abuser. If they can do this, they may be ready to adopt a whole new identity. However, acceptance by the community may be a problem. Trust, once betrayed, does not easily return. There will be a lot of difficult adjustments in society and hurdles to be crossed. Abusers will need a lot of encouragement and support to meet these many changes. Usually, ongoing counseling for former abusers, as well as for the family to whom they return, will be vital.

Restitution

The final step of healing has to do with trying to make things right. Indeed, such an idea may seem like an impossibility. How could all that extensive damage ever be repaid? There are some valuable things a former abuser can do to help the victim. The first thing he or she can do is to express to the victim complete acceptance of the blame for everything that happened, apologize sincerely, and approve of the victim's disclosure that brought his or her crime to light. This helps the victim to see that his or her own feelings were real and the anger justified. The next step is for the abuser to make a serious and long-term commitment to therapy and to inform the victim of this. The former abuser can support the family emotionally by allowing them to express their bitterness and anger without inflicting further pain by judging them for their feelings or getting angry with them. The offer of payment for the victim's needed therapy would also be very appropriate whenever possible.[17]

Summary

If we have learned nothing else about perpetrators of sexual abuse, one thing is clear: They have a multitude of problems. Most of them are struggling with the long-term effects of their own abuse, as well as the consequences of their own actions as abusers. A large part of their treatment is rather similar to that of survivors of abuse. Some is different. None of it is easy. There are many places where the abuser can get stuck in his or her progress, because the road back to health is a very long and perilous journey.

Abusers of others are indeed very needy people. At the same time, they have committed crimes against small children. Jail terms fulfill the need of society for punishment for criminal acts against innocent children. Unfortunately, jail does not resolve the personal issues behind the crime. We have to come to grips with the fact that we have a major problem in our society that needs to be corrected: the exploitation of innocent children. The number of victims is far too great to be ignored. The cycle must be stopped, but this will not be accomplished simply by jail alone. Nor will a simple act of forgiveness by the victim or society do the job. A complete change must take place within the abuser. The abuser must squarely face the truth of his or her own actions, understand its origins, and make things right within himself or herself and with the victims of the crime.

Wherever possible, the goal in treating abusers should be not only justice and punishment for their crimes, but also restoration as responsible, decent human beings, ready to take the responsibilities of life and healthy living, never to abuse again, and possibly to be able to help other abusers toward healing. Getting an abuser to this point would be one more giant step toward breaking the cycle of childhood sexual abuse.

Part 6

Can Anything Good Come from All of This?

14

Destination

The Plus Side of Trauma

"For I know the plans I have for you," declares the LORD, *"plans to prosper you and not to harm you, plans to give you hope and a future. Then you will call upon me and come and pray to me, and I will listen to you. You will seek me and find me when you seek me with all your heart. I will be found by you," declares the* LORD, *"and will bring you back from captivity."*

Jeremiah 29:11–14

Do you mean to tell me that something good could possibly come out of the trauma and horrible experiences of childhood sexual abuse? What of value could possibly come from all the shame, self-hatred, fear, anger, and hurt? What about all the years of doubt, uncertainty, and confusion, never knowing what is normal, groping one's way through life? Or the years of social insecurity, embarrassment for the blunders, misjudgment of character, intimidation by others? Do you mean to tell me something positive can come out of all of that?

Yes, I am happy to tell you that there are several positives that arise from trauma, suffering, and struggle in life. I see the journey as something like a mountain climber who is about to take on the challenge of a great and high mountain few others have climbed. The actual task of scaling the heights is a very difficult and arduous undertaking. There are many challenges to face. There will be sheer cliffs where there is little to hang on to. There are the hazards of

loose rock that may come tumbling down or undermine
the climber's footing. There are few easy stretches. As the
climber goes higher, the air gets colder, and weather becomes an ever-increasing hurdle. Snow may become haz-
ardous and blinding. Avalanches become a threat. Just the
hard work involved in pulling oneself up inch by inch, hour
by hour, day by day can get very tedious. Bones get weary;
sleep becomes fitful; the food is dull and uninteresting. The
further from the base of the mountain, the dizzier the
heights. Making one's way upward is difficult indeed.

Once the mountain climber has reached the top, however, all the sweat, fear, discouragement, and personal sacrifice are quickly forgotten. A new exhilaration takes over.
"I have reached my destination! I have made it to the top of
a world that few have attained! I have gotten to where I
want to be. I can shout with pride that I have conquered this
hurdle. I can rejoice in my accomplishment!"

Survival Skills

One of the distinct positives gained by the struggle to overcome childhood sexual abuse is the *ability to survive*. As I
work with survivors, I find people who have faced terrible,
extremely frightening, sometimes brutal, and even bizarre
and disgusting abuse that most of us cannot even imagine.
What is amazing is that they have survived. They have managed to get through it. They not only lived to tell about it
but keep on going in spite of their difficulties. Struggle has
become a familiar experience, an everyday task to be
worked out. Therefore, when major difficulties do come
their way, they are able to keep on surviving. They already
have the needed skills to work through the crisis.

Take, for example, another person who has had a relatively normal life, no real upheaval or really serious problems, comes from a secure family where love is expressed,
protection is provided, and life is generally comfortable and
even enjoyable. Now add a major crisis to the equation—for

certainly no one is exempt from the complications of life. Suppose the breadwinner parent is suddenly killed in an accident. The family is now in shock. Their financial security is knocked out from under them. They face some tough times ahead. Children who had their college expenses assured now are not sure how they can possibly reach their goal. They find themselves in a different situation socially where many of their supposed friends are no longer sure how to relate to them. They no longer have two parents like most of their friends. Now, because Mother has to work long hours to keep the family going, the closeness of the family seems fractured. What about the gnawing fears that some other devastating crisis could happen and make matters even worse? The going is tough for a long time, as there is no previous experience to draw from and few others to call on for help. The crisis looms very large. Life no longer seems secure and positive but seems dangerous and threatening.

Survivors of childhood sexual abuse have suffered serious atrocities as a child. When other life experiences come along that might well be devastating to others, abuse survivors view the new problems as somewhere close to normal. They have had plenty of experience at not being in control of their lives and have learned to live with it. One more day, one more problem. One day at a time. *Survivors are well acquainted with tough times and have an inner core of strength and character that few others have.* They are well experienced in the loneliness that comes from being misunderstood. No one knows the extent of their real struggle; they carry most of it alone. Survivors of abuse have been down most of these roads already and have developed the necessary skills to get them through.

Different Values

Survivors of childhood sexual abuse are on a different wavelength than most of their peers. Somehow chitchat about last night's football game, hockey scores, Wall Street quotations, Cindy's operation, or the latest television talk show do not hold their interest. They are more serious minded and more at ease discussing deeper issues. They are busy making sense out of life itself, focused on their families, friends, and relationships.

During the years of their abuse, survivors had to grow up fast. There was no carefree period of their lives. They were forced into adult experiences at a very young age. Even when there were chances to run out and play with other kids, their minds may have been too confused and preoccupied with all the trauma of their abuse to enter into the world of child's play. Because so much of life was a struggle, they thought serious thoughts. They did what they had to do against many odds. Some retreated within themselves; others exploded outwardly into aggressive behavior.

Still another group of survivors became very determined to somehow rise above all of this. They have doggedly pushed forward to make a better life for themselves and their families. They have determined never to hurt anyone else as they themselves have been hurt. They have not allowed themselves to get stuck in whining and complaining, looking for sympathy, or acting the part of a helpless victim. They have steadfastly looked toward a goal of a better life and have worked relentlessly to reach it. *They have come to value positive and healthy relationships and solid family life as their most important goal.*

An old saying states, "No one on their deathbed ever wished they had spent more time at the office." That statement simply underlines the fact that the satisfactions of our careers, the wealth we may derive, the power and control we may gain in our communities amount to nothing if we have not invested in positive relationships with our families and friends. Many don't find out until too late what really is important. Survivors of abuse have had to think that through already. They easily see through the hypocrisy of supposedly trustworthy and respectable people who became their abusers. Most survivors don't want to become like those models and, therefore, have carefully thought through just what they want in life and how to obtain it. And they will find ways to make it happen. They want lives built on honesty, decency, and a deep respect for the lives of others. Their goal is to build families where love is true, sincere, and nonmanipulative. They want to raise kids who understand the value of other people and are sensitive to others who hurt. Survivors already know the really important values of life.

Integration of Life Experiences

An integral part of the healing process is that of moving from victim stage to that of integrating life experiences. As the survivor has been able to put together the cause and effect of his or her abuse with the consequent emotional struggles of many years and released feelings that have been long locked up within, a new freedom begins to develop. Now the survivor is able to let feelings flow normally. Love, caring, and happiness become new experiences. The old mountains of self-hate, shame, rage, and deep hurt fade into the background. The high walls of guardedness and self-defense have been reduced to normal levels. A whole new freedom of expression has become a way of life, never before experienced.

The tremendous value of that new freedom may be difficult for another to grasp. We have been so accustomed to being free to say or feel the positive things in life that we don't prize that gift highly enough. The survivor knows the difference and likes to savor as much of that freedom as possible. *Freedom has become very valuable, and the survivor will guard it carefully, being very ready to defend against any situation or persons who may want to limit that freedom by their own need for power or control.*

The survivor will value highly every accomplishment and milestone along the way. In the past, there seemed little hope for a normal life. Any accomplishment was buried under an avalanche of problems to be overcome. As the survivor finds a way to integrate his or her experiences into life, each goal attempted and accomplished becomes a triumph worthy of celebration. Each new positive friendship established becomes extremely valuable and cause for rejoicing. Each victory in everyday living is a cause for thanksgiving. *Life itself becomes very valuable.*

Once real healing has taken place, that troubled focus changes. The survivor actually gets to a point in personal growth where the abuse becomes only one event in his or her life, and no longer the main event. The abuse with all its horrors has faded into the background. True, it never entirely goes away; some scars will always remain. But the abuse no longer occupies center stage. Because the past has been resolved, there is no need to dwell on it any longer. "Yes, it happened. The struggle was difficult. But I made it through. Let me celebrate life, love, freedom, and wholesome sexuality from here on."

Helping Others

Survivors of abuse are very sensitive to others who hurt. They know what it means to hurt deeply, and they can sense hurt in others. For this reason, many survivors have friends who have also been through abuse. Some survivors may still be too deeply into their own troubles to be of much help to another. Once the healing process has taken place, however, many survivors feel a special empathy for others who hurt, and want to help. Who can help better than someone who has been there, who knows the way, the sweat, the hard work, the discouraging times that go with the healing process?

My friends know that I love to fish in the wide-open spaces of saltwater, both bay and ocean. Fishing, or should I say *catching* fish, is more complicated than it seems. You have to know where the fish are, what kind of bait they are taking, whether they stay deep or shallow, whether they hide around bottom structure or run in the open. Water temperature, time of day, tides, and wind speed and direction all affect what happens. When I venture to a new area, I don't depend on my own abilities. I find someone who knows the local situation well and willingly pay them to take me where I need to go and help with the right equipment. And it works! I have many pleasant memories of successful excursions, not to mention countless meals of tasty fresh fish. I even have the pictures to prove it.

The survivor of abuse needs someone who knows the way—someone who has been there, who knows every step and has the experience and training necessary to help others find their way also. Someone looking for help will be attracted to a person who has been there, has found the way back, and has the compassion and patience to help another. Any survivor with a compassionate heart will attract fellow survivors and will have the unique opportunity to help them in their journey also.

I believe that God does allow some of us to experience difficult things in life so that we can eventually help others who struggle and thus multiply many times over the help that we might never have been able to give. As a survivor myself, I came to realize that *we have a unique ministry of healing.* One day the real message of this Scripture passage dawned on me:

Praise be to the God and Father of our Lord Jesus Christ, the Father of compassion and the God of all comfort, who comforts us in all our troubles, so that we can comfort those in any trouble with the comfort we ourselves have received from God.

2 Corinthians 1:3

Suddenly there it was—a whole new way for God to make something beautiful out of trauma. Because of the life experiences that had come to me personally, and because of

God's sustaining grace through it all, I could now be in a special position to help others also.

Although many survivors will need professional help, not all will get it. Some are too fearful; others don't believe they can afford the expense. If perhaps you are a survivor who has found help for yourself, you are in an excellent position to encourage and help others who struggle. They desperately need your support, encouragement, acceptance of their story and their feelings, and respect for confidentiality. A helping hand will be much appreciated. Not many are reaching out to help. As a fellow survivor you will have instant rapport and can be of tremendous assistance in a way that no one else can. A ministry of healing can be yours as a fellow survivor if you are willing to be available to those who hurt, to listen, learn, understand, accept, and encourage others in their struggle.

The Grace of God

It has been well said, "A doctor can give medicine, but God does the healing." None of us can make another well. The best trained therapist in the world cannot take a tangled life and straighten it all out again. The therapist can only bring certain abilities and expertise to the situation. Understanding of psychology and human behavior along with the useful technical skills are important, to be sure, but all the skills in the world do not make anyone grow. Probably the most important ingredient the therapist will provide is that of consistent caring and integrity, providing the atmosphere and nurturance to facilitate growth.

I can put a seed in the ground, but I cannot cause it to spring to life. Yes, I can add fertilizer, water, even provide some warmth, but I can't force it to grow. Stomping on the seed won't help; talking gently won't do much; chanting won't help either. The life is inside the seed. In matters of a broken heart from early abuse, neither you nor I can *make* the healing take place. The real growth comes from within the person, and *the genuine, solid, long-lasting healing comes from God.* The spiritual dimension of healing cannot be effectively bypassed or replaced by the finest technology in the world!

All of us are spiritual beings, whether we want to admit it or not. Whether the focus of our worship is on God, on money and power, on science, or on an atheistic view, which in essence worships man, we are all participating in some form of spiritual worship—the focus of our hope for the future. I am of the opinion that no complete healing takes place without the grace of God that reaches down and lifts us out of the quagmires of life. Medical science has come to realize that the inner strength of the person's spirit has a lot to do with a person's ability to heal. Only in recent years has psychology understood anything about the spiritual dimension in healing and the power of sincere forgiveness in the healing of the soul, which is a manifestation of the grace of God.

Jesus spent a large part of his ministry on the down and outers, society's rejects—people whom others considered weak, of little importance, the nobodies. The religious leaders of the day would have nothing to do with these people and objected to Jesus' attention to them. Jesus simply replied, "It is not the healthy who need the doctor, but the sick" (Matt. 9:12). God takes special delight in taking someone in desperate straits, who is at the bottom of life, who feels trapped and has nowhere to turn, and helping him or her out of the dark hole into a life of light and fulfillment. God doesn't start with the proud; he takes those who are loaded with shame, hurt, and self-loathing and makes them into something beautiful. An ordinary lump of coal, over time and under great pressure and adverse elements, can become a diamond. An oyster produces a priceless pearl that once started out as an irritant, a wound that needed to be healed. *God is in the business of making something out of nothing.* The apostle Paul wrote:

But God chose the foolish things of the world to shame the wise; God chose the weak things of the world to shame the strong. He chose the lowly things of this world and the despised things—and the things that are not—to nullify the things that are, so that no one may boast before him.

1 Corinthians 1:27–29

I don't know of any people who feel more like rejects, castoffs, or nothings than survivors of childhood sexual abuse. I'm not sure that survivors ever quite forget the past. They know what it means to be at the bottom, to feel like a worthless reject, for this is just how they felt about themselves for a very long time. Most survivors know where they have been and are so happy to have found freedom from their torment by facing the truth and pushing on. Yes, it was a lot of work, but no one ever did it all alone—God was there to help in the journey to health and wholeness. We may not have recognized God at work, but in the final analysis, God does the healing.

> Sally was obviously a very troubled person when she first came to my office. She was very depressed and quite withdrawn. She looked at the floor all the time. When she spoke of things troubling her, she buried her face in her knees, and spoke barely above a whisper. She was trying to fight her way back from a psychiatric hospitalization experience that she described as horrible. She was a dedicated Christian, very involved in Christian work with children. She had a number of memories of continued childhood sexual abuse, starting as an young child with her real father, then continued by a stepfather throughout her growing-up years, until she was finally able to leave home for further schooling at nineteen. It was the worst story of abuse that I had ever heard at the time. Her mother seemed oblivious to the whole thing, but she constantly isolated Sally from friends and community, not even allowing her out of the yard. Sally was truly trapped.

Sally had many problems. She trusted no one. She was on guard at all times. She always had a coat, even in the heat of summer, to keep herself covered. She would never visit the beach. She always sat in the back of the church near the door and was gone before church was over. She made herself as invisible as possible and spoke only when absolutely necessary. She went through many crisis experiences, especially in the first couple years of therapy. Any discussion of her history would put her into deep depression for the next three weeks; therefore, a very supportive therapeutic approach had to be used.

Although married a number of years with children, Sally was powerless to stand up for herself and did whatever the family demanded. Guilt and self-blame were constant overpowering forces. Every day of her life was an endless struggle just to survive. At times she despaired of life itself. During the course of her recovery she wore out three psychiatrists who said they could not help her anymore. In her distress, she twice became addicted to painkiller medicines but was able to shake off the habit.

Sally often spoke of a deep pain in her chest that did not fit anything medical, a pain so severe that she wished to stab the pain so it would go away. Whether she died as a result did not seem to matter that much, the pain was so terrible. She absolutely refused to see another psychiatrist. She was terrified of having to return to the hospital. A few times some definite limits had to be set on her dangerous behavior for the therapy to continue.

Her marriage to a very demanding and self-centered man eventually came apart. Sally became resigned to a life of singleness in which she had to sink or swim on her own. Her job was very stressful, and sometimes it was not clear whether she could continue, even though it was her livelihood. Somehow she pushed her way through, frequently just one step away from disaster. Although often tested to the limit, her Christian faith got her through the toughest areas.

Sally's therapy continued for a very long time. Although the improvement was hard to see from one month to the next and sometimes from one year to the next, there was definite measurable progress. No longer did she have her face in her knees nor talk with a whisper. She was able to sit and face me. She was able to dress more appropriately in hot weather, not needing the coat to cover herself. She had learned to deal with her supervisors at work and not allow herself to be constantly walked on. There were still multitudes of difficulties ahead, for she was still a fragile person.

Not long ago Sally came to my office bursting with good news. I had never seen her happy before. She was getting married! Because of her history, I wasn't sure whether this was good news or not. I felt better about it after I met her fiancé a few times. She seemed to have related to him positively as to no one else in her entire life. A few months after marriage, Sally realized she did not need to continue therapy. The troublesome nightmares of being chased and shot at were gone. She had found a husband who understood her needs, was kind and supportive, and knew how to encourage her as a person. This was the first experience in her life where she no longer felt exploited but instead was respected as a person in her own right. The crowning glory for her was the fact that after so many years of tremendous anxiety around all men and not wanting a man to touch her anywhere, she loved being cuddled by her husband and actually enjoyed sex in the marriage. "I never knew it could be so good!" she exclaimed. She was very happy. She was presently working on her socialization, and learning to open herself as a person to others. She was finally learning to celebrate life.

Sally realized that her ability to trust a man and her concept of the type of man she needed had come in a large part through our long association in therapy. But we both knew that her unwavering faith in God had a great deal to do with her recovery. Human means alone would not have gotten her to this point. She was a trophy of the grace of God at work. Sally had worked very hard at learning the survival skills and pursued the important things in life in spite of great odds. Yes, I had persevered when others had given up on her, but in the final analysis, God brought about the healing.

A Final Challenge

I wish to give a huge salute to the courage of all the Jills, Herbs, Janices, Riches, Jennifers, Bills, Sallys, Marjories, Sams, Phyllises, Matts, Susans, Joes, Bettys, Rons, Mary Anns, Sandys, Carolines, and an army of others not mentioned. Each of them has been through a tremendous amount of grief and suffering. But beyond that, they have wished to share their stories, wanting others to understand them and the countless others like them everywhere. Each one has taken an extra risk, fearful they won't be taken seriously or that they will be blamed or rejected as they have been so many times already. Since you have heard their stories, their challenge for you is to consider them carefully and to respond with open hearts and outstretched arms to receive them and other survivors at whatever stage of healing they may be. None of them need your criticism, judgment, or exclusion. They desperately need your caring, love, acceptance, time, and encouragement. Open your heart to them.

For other survivors who may be reading these words, they want to encourage you in your struggle also and to tell you there is healing and a good life ahead. They want you to know that the journey to health is sometimes difficult, but the rewards are great. They want you to find health and happiness also. They want you to see that you can have a useful and productive life.

To churches and church leaders everywhere they say, "You cannot afford to preach the love of God and ignore the suffering of so many right in your midst." If statistics are anywhere near correct, as many as 20 percent or more of your congregation have faced just such abuse. You may not know who they are, for they haven't yet identified themselves. They may be afraid of being judged as inferior Christians "because their faith isn't strong enough to leave it all in the past and get on with life." Survivors are turned off by churches that encourage everyone to act as though everything is wonderful when it isn't, when so many are dying inside and compassion is missing. Believe me, they would love to get on with their lives if it were that easy. Where can they turn if they cannot find acceptance, help, encouragement, and healing in the Christian church?

I wish to challenge individuals, churches, and caring communities everywhere to reach out to these people. Begin to think what your church can do to develop a ministry of caring to your own people. The church can:

- Begin to educate its people to needs right at our door and ways to begin to demonstrate the love of Christ.
- Have members meet with survivors on an individual basis to provide encouragement and modeling of a normal Christian life.
- Begin support groups where the participants can deal with the real problems of life.
- Supply reference resources to help survivors understand their struggle.
- Invite speakers for short conferences on recovery issues for all sorts of problems common to our society today.
- Begin to train members in the art of lay counseling and thus multiply the ministry of healing previously delegated only to the pastor and professionals.

- Help some survivors financially who can't afford the help they desperately need.

Once we have learned to walk a bit in the shoes of a survivor, the easy answers and judgmental attitudes fade away. (See appendix C for an in-depth look at ways the church can help survivors of sexual abuse.)

At the heart of Jesus' ministry was his message to the down and outers. That message was one of salvation but also one of healing and deliverance from the bitter struggles of life. Each of us must search our own hearts to see where our own priorities lie and how much of our lives are dedicated to those who hurt and are downtrodden. The words of Jesus as he spoke of the final judgment day give us perspective on what is really important in this life. Hear his challenge to each of us:

> Then the King will say to those on his right, "Come, you who are blessed by my Father; take your inheritance, the kingdom prepared for you since the creation of the world. For I was hungry and you gave me something to eat, I was thirsty and you gave me something to drink, I was a stranger and you invited me in, I needed clothes and you clothed me, I was sick and you looked after me, I was in prison and you came to visit me."
>
> Then the righteous will answer him, "Lord, when did we see you hungry and feed you, or thirsty and give you something to drink? When did we see you a stranger and invite you in, or needing clothes and clothe you? When did we see you sick or in prison and go to visit you?"
>
> Then the King will reply, "I tell you the truth, whatever you did for one of the least of these brothers of mine, you did for me."
>
> Matthew 25:34–40

What a perspective on life! Little things done for insignificant people lead to an eternal reward. And it can be yours as well.

The Mountaintop

The journey is complete. Just as the mountain climber looks from the lofty heights for miles around and soaks in the beauty of creation, so the survivor of abuse takes in the beauty of life never before experienced. The difficult steps of the perilous journey have faded into the background. New experiences of joy, peace, and satisfying relationships have come to the forefront. The faltering victim has become a survivor. The toughened and vigilant survivor has learned to master life as well as to relax and enjoy the good and the beautiful. Beyond that, the survivor is now ready to be a mountain guide for other victims who are struggling to find their way along the steeps and valleys of life.

Was it worth all that effort and difficulty? Any mountain climber will tell you, "Of course! The adventure and accomplishment make it all worthwhile, not to mention the beauty of the view from the top." The survivor of childhood sexual abuse who has gotten to the final destination will tell you the same. Was it worth all the hard work to get to the end? "You bet it was!" And would you want to go through it all with another who is struggling along the way? "Of course. Come with me, and let us travel through the mountains and valleys and over the rough trails together."

Appendix A

Survivor's Checklist

__✓__ 1. Fears related to darkness, such as being alone, sleeping alone, nightmares with themes of being chased, shot at, captured, or trapped.

__✓__ 2. Phobias to water, aversion to water in one's face, suffocation feelings, sensitivities to swallowing or gagging.

__✓__ 3. Hatred for one's body, view the body as ugly, hateful. Little attention to self-care, posture, appearance, or physical health.

__✓__ 4. Aversion to physical exposure: wears a lot of clothing even in summer, must be well covered at all times, needs absolute privacy in the bathroom.

__?__ 5. Addictive or compulsive behaviors: eating disorders, drug or alcohol usage, other addictions, repetitive actions driven by compulsions to do them.

__✓__ 6. Self-destructiveness: suicidal thoughts and attempts, self-abuse, self-cutting or mutilation attempts.

__✓__ 7. Phobias, such as intense fear of spiders, snakes, bridges, etc. Panic episodes for no apparent reason.

__✓__ 8. Depression: sometimes paralyzing, crying for no apparent reason, chronic feelings of hopelessness and failure.

__✓__ 9. Chronic anger: inability to recognize anger or express it, or constant anger and rage out of proportion to presenting events. Intense hostility toward an entire gender or ethnic group of the perpetrator.

___✓ 10. Inappropriate crisis response: overreaction (e.g., every stress is a crisis, emotional shock, shutdown, feelings of unreality), numbness of all feelings.

___ 11. Rigid control of one's thought process, always sober and humorless.

___✓ 12. Security-seeking behaviors, nervousness about being watched or surprised, easily startled.

___✓ 13. Trust issues: inability to trust others, indiscriminate trust, or total trust of everyone.

___✓ 14. Boundary issues: control, power, fear of losing control, obsessive-compulsive behaviors as a way of keeping control of oneself.

___✓ 15. Guilt, shame, low self-esteem, feeling worthless, easily embarrassed or humiliated.

_?_ 16. Victim pattern: allows self to be taken advantage of repeatedly, frequently sexual in relationships, no sense of own right or power to set limits, pattern of relationships with older persons.

___✓ 17. Feels a demand to achieve and be perfect in order to be loved. Strong need to be the giver, not the receiver.

___✓ 18. Fears of abandonment, rejection, and being ostracized by others.

___✓ 19. Memory blockage of early years or person or place.

___✓ 20. Feeling of carrying an awful secret: an urge to tell, fear of its being revealed, belief that no one will listen, generally secretive, feels a marked person.

___✓ 21. Feeling different from everyone else: may feel crazy, unreal, creating fantasy worlds.

___✓ 22. Denial: no awareness at all, minimizing of symptoms and evidence or severity, recall of only fragments of memories, not taking any of it seriously.

some 23. Sexual issues: sex in marriage feels dirty; strong aversion to particular sex acts or touch; trouble integrating sex and love; overlapping of affection, sex, dominance, aggression, and violence; difficulty with boundaries in sex, such as being promiscuous or frigid; must maintain control by being the aggressor or shut down completely; upset by orgasm; sexualizing of important relationships; sexual fantasies of dominance or being dominated.

√ 24. Intimacy problems: emotional closeness a problem, aversion to emotional vulnerability, relationships become conflicted, ambivalent hate-love combination.

√ 25. Limited tolerance for happiness, reluctance to trust happiness, and will withdraw from it.

This listing of questions is not complete but touches on the vital areas. If you find yourself or someone important to you identifying with a number of these questions, there is a strong likelihood that there has been some sort of molestation or sexual abuse in earlier years. Please explore this further with the help of a professional.

Note: Adapted from the "Incest Survivors' Aftereffects Checklist," in E. Sue Blume, *Secret Survivors* (New York: Ballantine Books, 1991), xxvii–xxx.

Appendix B

Finding a Good Therapist

If you need help in your own journey to healing, these guidelines may assist you as you choose a professional counselor or therapist.

1. Find a therapist who *shares your personal faith* or is at least supportive of your faith. Do not go to someone who is opposed to your faith or views your faith as a crutch. That person may do you more harm than good.

2. Look for someone with whom you feel *safe and comfortable.* You will need to feel as secure as possible as you dig into difficult material. Otherwise your anxiety will surely get in the way, causing progress to grind to a halt. Understand that even with the best of therapists there are times in the course of therapy where anxiety gets in the way, but that is usually a solvable problem as you discuss it with your therapist. But you need to have a general sense of safety and comfort. Discomfort with a particular therapist may well be a warning sign of future problems.

3. Choose someone *experienced in the area of recovery from childhood sexual abuse.* Someone who knows the journey well, an experienced guide, will be the best helper. The person needs to have the technical knowledge and empathy, as well as the ability to encourage, explain what is happening at different points in the process, and handle crisis times. He or she should also have a clear view of the journey that will bring you to the place of complete healing.

4. Should you think that you may have a *dissociative disorder*, which may or may not include Dissociative Identity Disorder or Satanic Ritual Abuse, ask if your therapist is experienced with that type of problem. Not all therapists are experienced enough in this relatively new area to be committed to the long and intense course of treatment required.

5. Find a *person of integrity who knows his or her own boundaries well.* Remember that as a victim of abuse, you are not strong in the relationship boundaries, especially with someone the same gender as your abuser. You need a therapist with a well-proven record. You need someone who is committed to keeping the boundaries clear and appropriate even when you are not sure yourself. Too many hurting people have sought counseling only to be sexually exploited by unscrupulous therapists, even ministers, seeking self-gratification for themselves at the expense of the client. The results are devastating. The damage takes years to repair.

    Most professional certifying agencies have a clear code of professional ethics their clinical members are required to follow, subject to dismissal. Some states have laws clearly defining sexual invasion of the client by the therapist as a criminal act. Should you unknowingly go to a therapist who wants to have a relationship of a sexual nature, either inside or outside of the therapy sessions, or who makes sexual suggestions to you, by all means *leave* and find a therapist who believes in and keeps clear boundaries. Seriously consider reporting the incident to the appropriate certifying agency.

6. Look for someone who is *honest and open*, is willing to take the time to answer your questions patiently, explains things for you, and treats you with respect. You want someone who is there to hear you, will accept what you have to say, and will keep the focus on your

problems and needs, not make excuses for your abuser or others who don't understand your needs.

7. Look for someone who has a *balanced view of both male and female issues*. A therapist who has not worked through his or her own issues and is either a man hater or a woman hater will not serve you well and may bias your own views.

8. *Check with others who are well satisfied with their therapists*. That can be one of your best recommendations.

Appendix C

Ways the Church Can Help

Professional therapists are not the only ones who can assist in the healing process. There is a great deal that interested Christians and churches can do to provide the atmosphere and sense of fellowship that fosters healing in others. Here are some suggestions:

1. *One-to-one-relationships.* As an individual, keep your eyes and ears open to those who may be in need in your congregation. Make it a special point to be genuinely friendly, open, and sincerely interested in others who are hurting. You may not automatically know who they are, but pay special attention to those who may seem to be quiet or reserved, stay on the outer edges of activities, and may be just a little bit different. Look for people you don't normally notice. Don't be pushy, but do go out of your way to greet them, and actively look for ways to engage in conversation. You may not get much response at first, but don't get discouraged. They want to know if you are sincere; they have been hurt too many times before. It will take time. Learn to share some of yourself with that person. As you build trust and a sense of acceptance with the survivor, he or she will feel encouraged to open more of himself or herself, and a relationship of healing may well begin.
2. *Church support groups.* Your church should seriously consider starting some support groups to meet different kinds of needs in your midst. Initially, "groups for

those who hurt" might be a good place to start. Later, the church may want to have more specific groups for specialized needs, such as recovery from abuse, alcoholism, eating disorders, grieving, etc. Professional leadership is not required, although it could be helpful to have a professional person as a resource for consultation as needed. A leader who is compassionate but has the ability to keep a group on an even keel can be very helpful. There are good materials available to use as study guides designed to help the participants bring out their thoughts and feelings. A good example would be a series by Dale and Juanita Ryan that includes individual workbooks on: *Recovery from Abuse, Shame, Fear, Image of Self, Alcohol, Spiritual Abuse, Grieving,* etc. (Downers Grove, Ill.: InterVarsity Press). The advantage of a group studying together in this way is that it helps those who hurt to realize they are not alone, that others can accept them with their problems, and they can be cared about by someone. The ability to share ourselves together and the experience of group affirmation causes some healing to take place. A sense of community can go a long way to heal old hurts.

3. *An abundance of resource materials.* The church library should be well stocked with books on current problems that we all face. There should be books and magazines that focus on recovery issues for the Christian that get to the real nitty-gritty of where people live, that give a wealth of information to help understand the problems, and that have practical guidance toward the path of recovery. Public mention of such materials should be made, not only to make people aware of what is available, but also to give the message that these are important issues in our church.

4. *Conferences on vital recovery subjects.* Invite a professional counselor, or someone well versed in this problem, to speak to your church or in some subgroups of

your church to further acquaint the congregation with what is happening around them. This will in turn encourage survivors in their own recovery issues. The church is thereby again giving the tangible message that we are interested in people who hurt, and we wish to help all we can.

5. *Training in encouragement and lay counseling.* The local congregation should seek out people who exhibit a heart of caring and encouragement who can be further trained and enlisted in the ministry of helping others. Invite a qualified professional to train your interested church people to enable them to develop skills in helping others in need. The same person may then be available for consultation and supervision of those involved in helping others. Someone will need to oversee the organization and operation of such a program. A pastor can thus multiply his effectiveness in meeting personal needs of his people, those involved in helping others will themselves grow tremendously, and those who benefit by such an effort will feel so much more a part of the congregation and a caring fellowship. I firmly believe that the church can and should be fulfilling such a ministry as part of the fellowship of believers intended by God—Christians ministering to other Christians, not leaving it all to the pastor and/or professional counselors who can only do part of the job.

A number of good, solid materials are available to draw from, both for the training of lay counselors and for the organization of such a program. Of particular interest in getting an overview of lay counseling is Siang-Yang Tan's *Lay Counseling: Equipping Christians for a Helping Ministry* (Grand Rapids: Zondervan, 1991).

6. *Referral sources.* Every church should have a list of professional therapists and counselors who are available when a referral is needed for someone in a great

deal of turmoil. Many survivors of childhood sexual abuse, especially where the abuse has been rather severe and at early ages, will need some professional help beyond what the church can supply. This is not a negative reflection on the church but simply a fact that this survivor's difficulties are deeply rooted and will require a lot of concentrated time and expertise, which are not available in the normal church ministry, to bring about healing. A few churches will have their own counseling service as part of the church ministry to the community.

7. *Financial assistance.* The local church should be willing to assist, at least on a partial basis, some who are desperately needy but who do not have the financial resources to get the help they need. A survivor who is barely able to function and in desperate financial straits is in just as much need as someone who is seriously ill but unable to pay the doctor bill or the rent. Don't pay the whole bill, but at least provide some of it where there is a genuine financial need.

Notes

Chapter 2: The Problem

1. C. Everett Koop, *The Surgeon General's Letter on Child Sexual Abuse* (Washington, D.C.: Department of Health and Human Services), 1–2.

2. Mic Hunter, *Abused Boys, the Neglected Victims of Sexual Abuse* (Lexington: D. C. Heath, 1990), 4.

3. Hunter, *Abused Boys*, 3.

4. The preceding entries are from Minnesota Program for Victims of Sexual Assault, *Biannual Report: Fiscal Years 1985–1986* (St. Paul: Minnesota Department of Corrections, 1987). Quoted by Hunter, *Abused Boys*.

5. Hunter, *Abused Boys*, 21–23.

6. A. B. Russell and C. Mohr-Trainor, *Trends in Child Abuse and Neglect: A National Perspective* (Denver: American Humane Association), 1984.

7. D. Russell, *The Secret Trauma: Incest in the Lives of Girls and Women* (New York: Basic Books, 1986).

8. L. Timnick, *Los Angeles Times*, 25 August 1985.

9. Committee on Sexual Offences against Children and Youths, *Sexual Offences against Children: Report of the Committee on Sexual Offences against Children and Youths* (Ottawa: Canadian Government Publishing Centre, 1984).

10. David Finkelhor, "The Sexual Abuse of Children: Current Research Reviewed," *Psychiatric Annals*, April 1967.

11. Grant L. Martin, *Counseling for Family Violence and Abuse*, Resources for Christian Counseling, ed. Gary R. Collins (Waco: Word Books, 1987), 147.

12. Hunter, *Abused Boys*, 34.

13. Martin, *Family Violence*, 148–49.

14. Phyllis P. Hart and Mary Rotzien, "Survey of Pastors and Counselors on Incest" (paper presented at the Christian Association for Psychological Studies, Dallas, May 1984).

15. Hunter, *Abused Boys,* 158–59.

16. Mary Sykes Wylie, "The Shadow of a Doubt," *The Family Therapy Networker,* September/October 1993, 29.

Chapter 3: Interruption of Normal Growth and Development in Early Childhood

1. David Finkelhor and Angela Browne, "The Traumatic Impact of Sexual Abuse: A Conceptualization," *The American Journal of Orthopsychiatry* (1985): 531–32.

2. E. Sue Blume, *Secret Survivors* (New York: Ballantine Books, 1991), 240.

Chapter 4: Early Childhood Effects: Pain and Anguish

1. Blume, *Secret Survivors.*

2. Hunter, *Abused Boys,* 80–81.

3. Finkelhor and Browne, "Traumatic Impact," 531–32.

Chapter 5: Later Effects in Adult Life: The Individual

1. American Psychiatric Association, *Diagnostic and Statistical Manual of Mental Disorders,* 4th ed. (Washington, D.C.: American Psychiatric Association, 1994), 320–22.

2. Blume, *Secret Survivors.*

3. *Merriam Webster's Collegiate Dictionary,* 10th ed., "anxiety."

4. Hunter, *Abused Boys.*

Chapter 6: Later Effects in Adult Life: Relationships

1. Finkelhor and Browne, "Traumatic Impact."

Chapter 7: Recognizing the Problem

1. Each of these definitions is adapted from *A Psychiatric Glossary* (Washington, D.C.: American Psychiatric Association, 1964).

2. James G. Friesen, *Uncovering the Mystery of MPD* (San Bernardino, Calif.: Here's Life Publishers, 1991), 62–63.

Chapter 8: Dissociative Identity Disorder

1. Friesen, *Uncovering the Mystery of MPD.*

2. *Diagnostic and Statistical Manual of Mental Disorders,* 477.

3. Adapted from Frank W. Putnam, *The Diagnosis and Treatment of Multiple Personality Disorder* (New York: Guilford Press, 1989), 106–14.

4. Putnam, *Diagnosis and Treatment*, 115.

5. David K. Sakheim and Susan E. Devine, *Out of Darkness* (New York: Lexington Books, 1992), 30–31.

6. Sakheim and Devine, *Out of Darkness*, 31.

7. Robert J. Lifton, *Thought Reform and the Psychology of Totalism* (New York: W. W. Norton, 1961), 68.

8. Sakheim and Devine, *Out of Darkness*, 31–32

9. Sakheim and Devine, *Out of Darkness*, 32.

10. Lifton, *Thought Reform*, 69–72.

11. Sakheim and Devine, *Out of Darkness*, 24–26.

12. *The Family Therapy Networker* is a bimonthly magazine addressing issues dealt with by family therapists (8528 Bradford Rd., Silver Spring, MD 20901).

13. Wylie, "Shadow of a Doubt," 18–73.

14. See inset in Wylie, "Shadow of a Doubt," 23.

15. Wylie, "Shadow of a Doubt."

16. See inset in Wylie, "Shadow of a Doubt," 27.

Chapter 9: The Confessional Process

1. Dan B. Allender, *When Trust Is Lost* (Grand Rapids: Radio Bible Class Discovery Series, 1991), 15.

Chapter 10: Facing the Enemy Within

1. Allender, *Trust Is Lost*, 21.

2. Allender, *Trust Is Lost*, 23–24.

3. Allender, *Trust Is Lost*, 24.

4. For a helpful discussion of the differences of persecutor alters and demons, see Friesen, *Uncovering the Mystery of MPD*, 221–23.

Chapter 11: Facing the Enemy Outside

1. Allender, *Trust Is Lost*, 27.

2. Allender, *Trust Is Lost*, 29.

Chapter 12: Protecting One's Own Family

1. Perry L. Draper, *Parents, Take Charge!* (Wheaton: Tyndale House, 1982), 9–10.

2. Draper, *Take Charge!* 150.

3. Draper, *Take Charge!* 150.

4. Draper, *Take Charge!* 163–68.

5. Adapted from a flyer produced by Health and Welfare, Canada.

Chapter 13: About Abusers

1. Miriam Horn, "Memories Lost and Found," *U.S. News & World Report,* 29 November 1993, 60.

2. Martin, *Family Violence,* 158–60.

3. *A Psychiatric Glossary* (Washington, D.C.: American Psychiatric Association, 1964). Sociopath: A person whose behavior is predominantly amoral, antisocial, or characterized by impulsive, irresponsible actions, satisfying only immediate and self-centered interests without concern for obvious and implicit social consequences accompanied by minimal outward evidence of anxiety or guilt.

4. Martin, *Family Violence,* 212–13.

5. Martin, *Family Violence,* 219.

6. Martin, *Family Violence,* 219–20.

7. Suzanne M. Sgroi, ed., *Handbook of Clinical Interventions in Child Sexual Abuse* (Lexington: D. C. Heath, 1982), 215–18.

8. Sgroi, *Clinical Interventions,* 216.

9. Adapted from Sandra L. Ingersoll and Susan O. Patton, *Treating Perpetrators of Sexual Abuse* (Lexington: Lexington Books, 1990), 16–19.

10. As reported by Heidi Vanderbilt, "Incest, a Chilling Report," *Lear's Magazine,* February 1991, 60–61.

11. Vanderbilt, "Incest," 62.

12. Vanderbilt, "Incest," 62.

13. Vanderbilt, "Incest," 63.

14. Eliana Gil, *Children Who Molest: A Guide for Parents of Young Sex Offenders* (Walnut Creek, Calif.: Launch Press, 1987), 8.

15. Gil, *Children Who Molest,* 8–9.

16. Gil, *Children Who Molest,* 10–13.

17. Adapted from Ingersoll and Patton, *Treating Perpetrators,* 40–67.

Bibliography

Allender, Dan B. *When Trust Is Lost.* Grand Rapids: Radio Bible Class Discovery Series, 1991.

Blume, E. Sue. *Secret Survivors.* New York: Ballantine Books, 1991.

Committee on Sexual Offences against Children and Youths. *Sexual Offences against Children: Report of the Committee on Sexual Offences against Children and Youths.* Ottawa: Canadian Government Publishing Centre, 1984.

Draper, Perry L. *Parents, Take Charge!* Wheaton: Tyndale House, 1982.

Finkelhor, David. "The Sexual Abuse of Children: Current Research Reviewed." *Psychiatric Annals,* April 1967.

Finkelhor, David, and Angela Browne. "The Traumatic Impact of Child Sexual Abuse: A Conceptualization." *American Journal of Orthopsychiatry,* 1985.

Frank, Jan. *A Door of Hope.* San Bernardino, Calif.: Here's Life Publishers, 1987.

Friesen, James G. *Uncovering the Mystery of MPD.* San Bernardino, Calif.: Here's Life Publishers, 1991.

Gil, Eliana. *Children Who Molest: A Guide for Parents of Young Sex Offenders.* Walnut Creek, Calif.: Launch Press, 1987.

Hart, Phyllis P., and Mary Rotzien. "A Survey of Pastors and Counselors on Incest." Paper presented at the Christian Association for Psychological Studies, Dallas, May 1984.

Heiman, Marsha. "Untangling Incestuous Bonds: The Treatment of Sibling Incest." In *Siblings in Therapy,* edited by M. Kahn and K. Lewis. New York: W. W. Norton, 1988.

Horn, Miriam. "Memories Lost and Found." *U.S. News & World Report,* 29 November 1993.

Hunter, Mic. *Abused Boys, the Neglected Victims of Sexual Abuse.* Lexington: D. C. Heath, 1990.

Ingersoll, Sandra L., and Susan O. Patton. *Treating Perpetrators of Sexual Abuse.* Lexington: Lexington Books, 1990.

Koop, C. Everett. *The Surgeon General's Letter on Child Sexual Abuse.* Washington, D.C.: Department of Health and Human Services.

Lifton, Robert J. *Thought Reform and the Psychology of Totalism.* New York: W. W. Norton, 1961.

Martin, Grant L. *Counseling for Family Violence and Abuse.* Resources for Christian Counseling. Edited by Gary R. Collins. Waco: Word, 1987.

Minnesota Program for Victims of Sexual Assault. *Biannual Report: Fiscal Years 1985–1986.* St. Paul: Minnesota Department of Corrections, 1987.

Psychiatric Glossary. Washington, D.C.: American Psychiatric Association, 1964.

Putnam, Frank W. *The Diagnosis and Treatment of Multiple Personality Disorder.* New York: Guilford Press, 1989.

Russell, A. B., and C. Mohr-Trainor. *Trends in Child Abuse and Neglect: A National Perspective.* Denver: American Humane Association, 1984.

Russell, D. *The Secret Trauma: Incest in the Lives of Girls and Women.* New York: Basic Books, 1986.

Ryder, Daniel. *Breaking the Circle of Satanic Ritual Abuse.* Minneapolis: CompCare Publishers, 1992.

Sakheim, David K., and Susan E. Devine. *Out of Darkness.* New York: Lexington Books, 1992.

Sgroi, Suzanne M., ed. *Handbook on Clinical Interventions in Child Sexual Abuse.* Lexington: D. C. Heath, 1982.

Tan, Siang-Yang. *Lay Counseling: Equipping Christians for a Helping Ministry.* Grand Rapids: Zondervan, 1991.

Vanderbilt, Heidi. "Incest: A Chilling Report." *Lear's,* February 1991.

Wylie, Mary Sykes. "The Shadow of a Doubt." *The Family Therapy Networker,* September/October 1993.